A HOLY AMBITION

TO PREACH WHERE CHRIST HAS NOT BEEN NAMED

Second Revised Edition

JOHN PIPER

Contents

Preface   3

Introduction—A Holy Ambition: To Preach   7
Where Christ Has Not Been Named

1. The Story of His Glory   17

2. Doing Missions When Dying Is Gain   37

3. The Voice of the Sovereign Shepherd   55

4. A Rescue Mission from Glory to Gladness   69

5. The Unsearchable Riches of Christ for All Peoples   85

6. Let the Peoples Praise You, O God! Let All   95
the Peoples Praise You!

7. The Aroma of Christ among the Nations   111

8. Cities of Ruthless Nations Will Fear the Lord   123

9. Gospel to the Nations, Generosity to the Poor   135

10. "I Am Sending You Out as Sheep in the Midst   147
of Wolves"

11. Music and Missions for the Glory of God   159

12. Missions Exists Because Worship Doesn't   171

Afterword—If I Could Start All Over: 181
Six Lessons for Your Twenties

Scripture Index   188

Preface

The title of this book comes from the apostle Paul. It has a special significance for me, because he was not young when he burned with his "holy ambition." I am not young. But my heart burns at age 73 with the ambition of pursuing God's global glory. For whatever time I have left, I want my life to count for the gladness of the nations in the glory of Christ. I hope this book makes your heart burn in the same way.

Paul said, "I make it my *ambition* to preach the gospel, not where Christ has already been named" (Romans 15:20). That's the heart of a missionary talking—a person whose calling is to herald the good news of Christ in places where people have no access to the gospel.

To be sure, there is always more great gospel work to be done in every church and every neighborhood in every nation of the world. Most Christians are meant to give their lives to this glorious work of shining with the light of

Christ in places already touched with the gospel. We know this because, when Paul told the Roman church about his ambition to go to Spain (Romans 15:24, 28), he did not invite the whole church to leave Rome and go with him.

Nevertheless, my prayer is that God would ignite a flame in some believers in every Christian church around the world—a *holy ambition* to pick up Paul's mantle, and take the gospel where it has never gone. We are publishing this revised edition of *A Holy Ambition* as one piece of kindling to throw on that flame.

In this edition, we have added four chapters of new material. We removed about a third of the original content, and freshly edited and organized the remainder. It's been eight years since the first edition appeared. Since then, my thirty-three-year pastorate at Bethlehem Baptist Church has come to an end. God designed and performed a beautiful transition for the church into new leadership.

But in this new chapter of life, as I work full-time for Desiring God and Bethlehem College & Seminary, the cause of world missions remains prominent. I have been able to travel internationally more than I used to, as we try to serve newer movements of gospel growth. And to my amazement, God gave me the privilege of being part of starting the CROSS missions conference for students.

This conference has grown from its first gathering in 2013, to 7,000 attenders in 2018. It is rooted in the conviction that people perish eternally if they do not hear and believe the good news of Christ's death and resurrection for sinners. It foregrounds the essential role of the local church. It stresses the truth that not every Christian is a missionary, but that missions is a special cross-cultural calling. It exults in the sovereignty of God's grace in raising to life people from every ethnicity who are spiritually dead. And it waves the flag that Christians care about all suffering, especially eternal suffering.

I mention the CROSS conference mainly to illustrate that God is willing to fulfill an old man's holy ambition. I stand amazed that I have been granted the privilege of joining with others in launching thousands of Christians into cross-cultural missions. If you are reading this book, you are not too young, or too old, to dream a new gospel dream.

I say this with the confidence that God can make your holy ambition clear to you. The reason for that confidence is that, when Paul wanted to explain his confidence in his holy ambition, he did not refer to his unrepeatable encounter with Christ on the Damascus Road. He referred to his eminently repeatable encounter with God's word in the Bible. In Romans 15:21, he explained his confidence with Isaiah 52:15,

> Those who have never been told of him will see,
> and those who have never heard will understand.

God warranted and clarified Paul's holy ambition with the Scriptures. He can do the same for you. I pray that this will happen as you read these chapters, which are saturated with God's word.

John Piper
Senior Teacher and Founder, Desiring God
Chancellor, Bethlehem College & Seminary

ROMANS 15:18-24

For I will not venture to speak of anything except what Christ has accomplished through me to bring the Gentiles to obedience—by word and deed, [19] by the power of signs and wonders, by the power of the Spirit of God—so that from Jerusalem and all the way around to Illyricum I have fulfilled the ministry of the gospel of Christ; [20] and thus I make it my ambition to preach the gospel, not where Christ has already been named, lest I build on someone else's foundation, [21] but as it is written, "Those who have never been told of him will see, and those who have never heard will understand." [22] This is the reason why I have so often been hindered from coming to you. [23] But now, since I no longer have any room for work in these regions, and since I have longed for many years to come to you, [24] I hope to see you in passing as I go to Spain, and to be helped on my journey there by you, once I have enjoyed your company for a while.

A Holy Ambition: To Preach Where Christ Has Not Been Named

Let's focus on three parts of this Romans 15 text. All three have direct implications for your life (even if you are currently not aware of them), and all of them relate directly to God and his purposes in the twenty-first century. I see, first, a holy ambition; second, an immeasurable need; third, a global strategy. Let's take these one at a time and see how they relate to each other and to us and to our world today.

A Holy Ambition

Romans 15:20 reads, "And thus I make it my ambition to preach the gospel, not where Christ has already been named, lest I build on someone else's foundation."

Paul was controlled by a holy ambition: He says in verse 22, "This is the reason why I have so often been hindered from coming to you." And he says at the end of verse 23, "I have longed for many years to come to you."

When you long to do something for years and years, but you don't do it, something or someone must be controlling you to the contrary. What was controlling Paul and keeping him from going to Rome? He was not finished with his ambition in the regions from Jerusalem to Illyricum. But finally, he says in verse 23, "I no longer have any room for work in these regions." And then in verse 24, "I hope to see you in passing as I go to Spain."

In other words, he was controlled by an ambition to preach the gospel to those who had not heard the name of Jesus from Jerusalem to Illyricum (modern-day Albania), and he would not turn from this ambition until it was fulfilled. But now the work is done in those regions, and his ambition is taking him to Spain. That frees him finally to do what he has wanted to do for years—namely, visit the church in Rome and enjoy their company for a little while.

It is a good thing to be controlled by a holy ambition. Are you controlled by a holy ambition? I am calling it *holy* because its aim is holy—to see people from all the nations who have never heard of Jesus believe in him and become obedient to him and be saved by him from their sin and from God's wrath. I am also calling this ambition *holy* because it comes from the holy God and his holy word, as we will see in a few moments. It is right and it is good to be controlled by a holy ambition.

Do you have a holy ambition? Not everyone *should* have Paul's ambition. One plants, another waters (1 Corinthians 3:6–8). Each has his own gift (1 Corinthians 7:7). Each stands or falls before his own master (Romans 14:4). But I think God would be pleased if each of his children had a holy ambition.

Holy Ambition for Girls and Boys

Little children, listen to me carefully for a moment. I know the words *holy ambition* are unusual and you don't use them every day. *Holy ambition* means something you *really* want to do that God wants you to do. Something you want to do so much that doing it keeps you from doing other things that you also really like to do. Paul really wanted to go to Rome for years. But he didn't go because he wanted something else more. He wanted to preach the gospel in Asia and Greece, where people didn't know about Jesus. He really, really, really wanted to do this. We call that kind of desire an *ambition*. And we call it a *holy ambition* when it is something God wants you to do too.

Do you have one? Probably not yet. You're still a child. That's what you're supposed to be. But some day you won't be a child anymore. And one of the differences between being a child and growing up is that growing up as a Christian means you get a holy ambition.

Most little girls, my Talitha included, really want to have and play with dolls. That's a good thing. But the day is going to come, little girls, when you will put away the fun of playing with dolls and grow up into the even bigger, better joy of caring for real babies in the nursery. And maybe you will even lead a ministry someday of caring for hungry babies far away, or lonely babies who have no mommy or daddy. And for some of you, this will become a holy ambition. For others, your holy ambition will be something else.

And boys, listen. If you are like I was, what you really want is a ball, a truck, or a gun, and somebody to play with. I've never had a real gun (except a pellet rifle). But I shot a lot of bad guys with my Matt Dillon pistol and my Lucas

McCain-like circle-handled rifle. I loved playing football with my friends and digging roads across the street for my trucks and drawing my pistol so fast you couldn't see it. It was fun. And that was good.

But some day you won't be a little boy any more. And one of the differences between being a little boy and growing up is that growing up as a Christian means you get a holy ambition. And that means the fun of guns and trucks and balls gets small and the joy of fighting for justice and salvation gets big. Growing up means getting a holy ambition to wield the sword of the Spirit mightily and drive a truckload of love to the needy and kick Satan's rear end in the name of Jesus.

Moms and dads, single people, young and old, all Christians should have a holy ambition—something you really, really want to do for the glory of God. It is something that controls you. It helps you decide not to go to "Rome" yet. It gives eternal focus, organization, and passion to your life.

The Source of Holy Ambition

Where does it come from? A crucial part of the answer is given in the link between Romans 15, verses 20 and 21: "Thus I make it my ambition to preach the gospel, not where Christ has already been named, lest I build on someone else's foundation, but *as it is written*, 'Those who have never been told of him will see, and those who have never heard will understand.'"

Now here is the amazing and relevant thing about this for us. We know from Acts 9 and 22 and 26 that Paul was called by the risen Christ on the Damascus road. Jesus gave Paul his mission in Acts 26:17-18: "I am sending you [to the nations] to open their eyes, so that they may turn from darkness to light and from the power of Satan to God, that they may receive forgiveness of sins and a place among those who are sanctified by faith in me." So he got a calling straight from the risen, living, all-sovereign Jesus Christ to be a light to the Gentiles.

But that's not what he says in Romans 15:21. He doesn't say, "I have this ambition to be a light to the nations who don't know Christ because Jesus called me on the Damascus road." He says, in effect, "I have this ambition—I am controlled by a passion to preach where Christ has not been named—because Isaiah 52:15 says, 'Those who have never been told of him will see, and those who have never heard will understand.'"

What do you make of that? Here's what I make of it. When Jesus called Paul on the Damascus road to take the gospel to the Gentiles who had never heard, Paul went to his Bible (what we today call the Old Testament) and looked for a confirmation and explanation of this calling to see how it fit into God's overall plan. And he found it. And for our sake he speaks this way. He doesn't refer just to his experience on the Damascus road, which we will never have. He refers to God's written word, which we *do* have, and he roots his ambition there.

So my answer to the question, "Where does your holy ambition come from?" is this: it comes from a personal encounter with the living Christ (not necessarily as dramatic as the Damascus road), shaped and informed and empowered by the written word of God. As you meditate on the law of the Lord day and night (Psalm 1:2)—as you immerse yourself in God's word—he comes and takes some truth of that word and burns it into your heart until it becomes a holy ambition. If that hasn't happened yet, saturate yourself with the word of God and ask him for it.

An Immeasurable Need

God doesn't lead us into ambitions that are pointless—that you will regret at the end of your life. There is always a need to be met (not a need in God, but in the world) by a holy ambition. Holy ambitions are not about self-exaltation. They are always a form of love. They always meet someone's need.

Now what is the immeasurable need Paul refers to in this text? Look at verse 20: "Thus I make it my ambition to preach the gospel, not where Christ has already been named." That means that Paul has set his face like flint to preach the gospel to people who have never heard of Christ. They don't even know his name.

Now here's the question: If these people don't even know Jesus's name, then are they responsible to believe on him for salvation? And if not, then wouldn't it be safer, for them, just to leave them in their ignorance and believe that God will have mercy on them and save them because they haven't heard of Jesus? Why, Paul, do you suffer so much to preach the gospel to people who have never heard the name of Jesus?

Paul gave the answer in Romans 1:18–23. Read it with me slowly and soberly and feel the weight of it the way Paul must have. These words are written about all those peoples and nations who have never heard the name of Jesus, and whom Paul is driving to reach with his holy ambition.

The wrath of God is revealed from heaven against all ungodliness and unrighteousness of men, who by their unrighteousness suppress the truth. For what can be known about God is plain to them, because God has shown it to them. For his invisible attributes, namely, his eternal power and divine nature, have been clearly perceived, ever since the creation of the world, in the things that have been made. So they are without excuse. [Those are the fatal words that define the immeasurable need Paul sees; the nations who have never heard of Jesus will have no excuse at the judgment day.] For although they knew God, they did not honor him as God or give thanks to him, but they became futile in their thinking, and their foolish hearts were darkened. Claiming to be wise, they became fools, and exchanged the glory of the immortal God for images resembling mortal man and birds and animals and creeping things.

Paul says in Romans 2:12, "All who have sinned without the law will also perish without the law, and all who have sinned under the law will be judged by the law." Everybody will be judged according to what they have access to. And everybody will perish who does not hear the gospel, because everybody suppresses the truth that they have and lives in rebellion against God. There is only one hope: hearing and believing the gospel of Jesus Christ.

The need of the nations who do not know the name of Jesus is an immeasurable need. It is an infinite need. The greatest need that can be imagined is the need of the nations to hear the gospel of Jesus Christ and believe. Because the gospel of Jesus "is the power of God for salvation to everyone who believes, to the Jew first and also to the Greek" (Romans 1:16). And no one is saved without it.

Not every one of you is called to go like Paul. But you can't be a loving person and not want your life to count or contribute to the meeting of this great need.

A Global Strategy

But God is calling some of you to join Paul personally and vocationally in this particular global strategy. Here's the strategy. And it is amazing.

Here are Paul's amazing statements. First, verse 19: "From Jerusalem and all the way around to Illyricum I have fulfilled the ministry of the gospel of Christ." That's from Jerusalem up through Syria, across Asia Minor (Turkey), down through Greece on the east side and up the west to northern Italy where Albania is today. Paul says he has fulfilled the gospel there. And he underlines that astonishing statement in verse 23 by saying, "I no longer have any room for work in these regions." And then in verse 24 he says, "I go to Spain."

What in the world did he mean that he had no room for work from Jerusalem to Illyricum? It is not a risk to say that there were tens of thousands of people yet to be evangelized in those regions. We know this because Paul writes to Timothy at Ephesus (in this very region) and commands him to "do the work of an evangelist" (2 Timothy 4:5). In other words, there are people who need to be evangelized. And Paul says his work is done in this region.

I take that to mean that Paul is not a local evangelist;

he's a frontier missionary, a pioneer missionary. That is, his calling and his ambition is not to do evangelism where the church has been planted. The church should do that. Paul's calling and his ambition is to preach the gospel where there is no evangelizing church. Where there are no Christians. Where they don't even know what a Christian is.

The label for the role is not what's crucial. What's crucial is the distinction. There are frontier (or pioneer) missionaries, and there are evangelists. Missionaries cross cultures and learn languages. And *frontier* missionaries pour out their lives "by word and deed, by the power of signs and wonders, by the power of the Spirit of God" (Romans 15:18–19) to break through thousands of years of darkness and the reign of Satan over a people who do not know the King of kings and the Savior of the world.

This was Paul's ambition. And since the Great Commission to make disciples of all nations is still valid, and there are peoples today who do not know the gospel, every church should pray that God would raise up many frontier missionaries and make all of us evangelists.

I can imagine—indeed, I pray—that ten years from now, someone will write a letter home from an unreached people and say, "I am here to speak the gospel to those who have never heard, for as it is written in Romans 15:20, 'I make it my ambition to preach the gospel, not where Christ has already been named, lest I build on someone else's foundation.' God burned that word onto my heart and turned it into a holy ambition."

Lord, please do that. Amen.

EPHESIANS 1:3-6

Blessed be the God and Father of our Lord Jesus Christ, who has blessed us in Christ with every spiritual blessing in the heavenly places, [4]even as he chose us in him before the foundation of the world, that we should be holy and blameless before him. In love [5]he predestined us for adoption to himself as sons through Jesus Christ, according to the purpose of his will, [6]to the praise of his glorious grace, with which he has blessed us in the Beloved.

1

The Story of His Glory

Human beings, by nature, don't draw the same conclusions that God does from many facts, and in our human nature we don't feel the same way God does about the conclusions that he draws from the facts.

By *human nature* I mean a mind, an attitude, a bent that thinks badly about many things. "By nature [we are] children of wrath" (Ephesians 2:3). By our very nature, there is something wrong with us. We don't just do bad *things*; we have a bad *nature*, often doing terrible things with the abilities God has given us. Another text would be 1 Corinthians 2:14: "The natural person does not accept the things of the Spirit of God, for they are folly to him."

If God says something strange, we don't like it. We, by nature, regard lots of things that are true as foolish. So there's something wrong with us: when God draws conclusions that look strange to us, we get in his face and we disagree with him and call him into question.

God's Motive for Missions

The older I get, the more I see evidences of this in me and in other Christians in the way we read our Bibles and in the way we respond to providences. For example, in order for us to have a heart for unreached peoples that is strong enough, deep enough, durable enough, God-centered enough, and Christ-exalting enough to be the kind of heart it should be, we need to base this heart for the nations on the same foundation on which God bases his heart for the nations. But when we see what God bases his heart for the nations on, many people start to get uncomfortable, because God bases his heart for the nations on *his passion for his own name and his own glory.*

I go all over the country and the world saying this, and then I watch the reactions and field the questions. I have discovered, for about thirty years now, that God's jealousy for his own name as he saves and judges the nations is alien to many believers, not to mention unbelievers. Since that is so alien to us, I want to build the case that God bases his heart for the nations on his heart for himself.

In doing that, I want to lay out texts, because what *I* think is of no consequence whatsoever if it doesn't correspond to biblical truth. The only thing you should care about is if what I say corresponds to what the Bible teaches. That's all that matters. My authority as a pastor isn't what counts, my being older than most readers isn't what counts, my having a certain level of education isn't what counts. What counts is this: Does this man get under the Bible instead of over the Bible? Does he submit and then talk plainly about what he finds here, in such a way that ordinary folks can say, "Yes, that must be what it says and what it means, because there it is"?

God's Ultimate Goal

God's heart for the nations is built on God's heart for God. God's zeal to reach the nations with the glory of his Son and save sinners is built on his zeal that his name be exalted in and through the worshiping of Christ. That's the argument. And the way to argue for it, I think, is to simply look at an array of texts that show that God does everything for the sake of magnifying his glory.

Here's my thesis: God's ultimate goal in creation and redemption is to uphold and display his glory for the enjoyment of his redeemed people from every tribe and tongue and people and nation. God's main goal, his ultimate goal, is to uphold and display his glory. That is the seemingly offensive thing to many people. It just sounds so self-centered and self-exalting to many people.

The key to why God's self-exaltation—that is, the pursuit of the magnifying of his own glory—is not vicious but virtuous, not unloving but loving, is this word *enjoyment*. He is doing it for the enjoyment of his people. If God did not preserve and exalt his glory, we would not be given the very thing that we were designed to be most satisfied by—namely, God and his glory. He is the one being in the universe for whom self-exaltation is the highest virtue and the greatest act of love. When you stand in front of God, if you're thinking God's thoughts and not the world's thoughts, what you want is for God to say, "Hey, stand in front of me and watch *this!*" And then you want him to be God, in the fullness of his grace and justice, so that you can spend eternity enjoying him and going deeper into him.

Consider Isaiah 28:5: "In that day the Lord of hosts will be a crown of glory, and a diadem of beauty, to the remnant of his people." What will it mean that he will be a crown of glory? Whose head will it be on? He's the crown. He is not the head. It's going to be on your head. Take a deep breath. He will be a crown of glory and a diadem of beauty. In other words, he will satisfy every longing you have for glory and beauty. Everything good that you ever longed for will be satisfied in him.

Therefore, it is loving for him to lift himself up and say, "Here I am, world! Admire!" If you did that, you would be unloving, because you are not all-satisfying. He is. You should simply go all over the world pointing to him. Say, "World, look!" Look at Christ especially, because there, when Christ died, the glory of the grace of God was magnified, which is the apex of all his glory, which is why Christ is the center of everything.

To the Praise of His Glorious Grace

The texts we are going to look at will appear in chronological order. This first passage describes an event that was chronologically first in the universe—no, first in reality, even *before* the universe. Look at Ephesians 1.

> Blessed be the God and Father of our Lord Jesus
> Christ, who has blessed us in Christ with every
> spiritual blessing in the heavenly places, even
> as he chose us in him before the foundation of

the world, that we should be holy and blameless before him. In love he predestined us for adoption to himself as sons through Jesus Christ, according to the purpose of his will, to the praise of his glorious grace, with which he has blessed us in the Beloved. (Ephesians 1:3–6)

I'll paraphrase that: God, before the foundation of the world, set his heart on being praised. Choosing, predestining, adopting—these are all means to that ultimate goal. And the goal is, the purpose is, that we *praise his glorious grace*, which was supremely manifested in Jesus, and which was planned before the foundation of the world.

So there's my first argument: From the beginning, before we existed, God's design was to get praise for his glorious grace.

Images Are Created to Image

The next item in my chronology is creation.

Then God said, "Let us make man in our image, after our likeness. And let them have dominion over the fish of the sea and over the birds of the heavens and over the livestock and over all the earth and over every creeping thing that creeps on the earth." So God created man in his own image, in the image of God he created him; male and female he created them. (Genesis 1:26–27)

What does it mean to be created in the image of God? Books by the hundreds have been written on the *imago dei*, as it's called. It's a huge issue. Is it our reason? Is it our

emotions? Is it that we have moral accountability? How
are we like God?

I'm going to avoid the whole controversy and say
something much simpler: images are created to image.
Why do you ever set up an image of anything? To image it!
If someone puts up a statue of Stalin, he wants people to
look at Stalin and think about Stalin. If someone puts up
a statue of George Washington, he wants people to look at
it and think about the founding fathers. Images are made
to image. So if God made us, unlike all the other animals,
in his image, whatever it means in detail, this it means
clearly: God is the reality, and we are the image. Images
are created to set forth the reality.

Why did God create man? To show God! He created
little images so that they would talk and act and feel in a
way that reveals the way God is—so that people would
look at the way you behave, the way you think, the way you
feel, and say, "God must be great. God must be real." *That*
is why you exist. God didn't create you as an end in yourself. *He's* the end, and you're the means. And the reason
that's such good news is because the best way to show that
God is infinitely valuable is to be supremely happy in him.
If God's people are bored with God, they are really bad
images. God is not unhappy about himself. He is infinitely
excited about his own glory.

That's why the Son received the words "This is my
beloved Son, with whom I am well pleased" (Matthew
3:17). Take those words *well pleased*. God doesn't say he
feels just okay about Jesus. He is absolutely thrilled with
Jesus as the image of himself. So if we watch television,
go on the computer, handle money, and use food in a way
that communicates to the world that these things are our

treasure rather than God, that these things make us satisfied rather than God, then he's getting bad press and we're not doing what we were created to do. We were created to image God.

So, God predestined people *for* his glory, and he created people for the *display* of his glory.

God Acts for the Sake of His Name

Staying in chronological order, we'll now move to the exodus.

Thus says the Lord GOD: On the day when I chose Israel, I swore to the offspring of the house of Jacob, making myself known to them in the land of Egypt; I swore to them, saying, I am the LORD your God. ⁶On that day I swore to them that I would bring them out of the land of Egypt into a land that I had searched out for them, a land flowing with milk and honey, the most glorious of all lands. ⁷And I said to them, 'Cast away the detestable things your eyes feast on, every one of you, and do not defile yourselves with the idols of Egypt; I am the LORD your God.' ⁸But they rebelled against me and were not willing to listen to me. None of them cast away the detestable things their eyes feasted on, nor did they forsake the idols of Egypt. Then I said I would pour out my wrath upon them and spend my anger against them in the midst of the land of Egypt. ⁹But I acted for the sake of my name, that it should not be profaned in the sight of the nations among whom they lived, in whose sight I made myself known to them in bringing them out of the land of Egypt. (Ezekiel 20:5–9)

Here we begin to see something that's going to climax in the cross of Christ—namely, the ground of the deliverance of a rebellious people is God's jealousy for his name. If God, at this point, had not been supremely jealous for his name, wrath would have fallen upon the people of Israel: "Then I said I would pour out my wrath upon them and spend my anger against them in the midst of the land of Egypt" (v. 8).

That's what they deserved. But something checked that just disposition in God: "But I acted for the sake of my name, that it should not be profaned in the sight of the nations among whom they lived, in whose sight I made myself known to them in bringing them out of the land of Egypt" (v. 9).

To Make Known His Mighty Power

Get that principle. There are so many Christians today who see the salvation of God as an evidence of their worth instead of God's worth. That doesn't work here. It just doesn't work. When they walked through the sea on dry land, what should they say? "We must be really good!" No! They deserved wrath, and they got deliverance because God is really great, and he means to be known as great.

Here is the way Psalm 106:6–8 puts it:

Both we and our fathers have sinned; we have committed iniquity; we have done wickedness. Our fathers, when they were in Egypt, did not

consider your wondrous works; they did not
remember the abundance of your steadfast love,
but rebelled by the sea, at the Red Sea. Yet he
saved them for his name's sake, that he might
make known his mighty power.

Oh, how thankful I am for worship leaders who get this,
who are constantly saying, "We're going to glory in our
Redeemer!" We're not going to glory in the fact that God's
saving me must mean I am glorious. We're not going to
talk like that. That doesn't satisfy the soul. That's the carnal
mind using the cross to buttress its ego. There are many
people who do that, but the cross crucifies the ego and
puts all worth on Jesus and the Father.

Why Ten Plagues?

Now to the book of Exodus itself. God says, "I will harden
Pharaoh's heart, and he will pursue them, and I will get
glory over Pharaoh and all his host, and the Egyptians
shall know that I am the LORD" (Exodus 14:4).

Have you ever asked why God used ten plagues to
deliver Israel from Egypt instead of one? If you thought
like the world, you might think, "Well, he did his best for
nine, and then he really pulled the trump card at ten and it
worked." That's not the case, because we read at the beginning of the story that he was going to multiply his signs in
Egypt (Exodus 7:3–4). God *planned* to multiply his signs in
Egypt. Why? Because he meant to get glory over Pharaoh,
who was so against God. He meant to magnify himself.
The exodus, which is a pointer to our exodus from sin, was
based upon God's zeal for his name.

Healthy Jealousy

A few months after the exodus came the giving of the law.

> You shall have no other gods before me. You
> shall not make for yourself a carved image, or
> any likeness of anything that is in heaven above,
> or that is in the earth beneath, or that is in the
> water under the earth. You shall not bow down
> to them or serve them, for I the LORD your
> God am a jealous God, visiting the iniquity
> of the fathers on the children to the third and
> the fourth generation of those who hate me.
> (Exodus 20:3–5)

Have no gods before me because I'm jealous, God says.
What does *jealous* mean here? There is some jealousy
that is bad, and there is some jealousy that is good. I just
did some premarital counseling recently, and I looked at
some personality things that I saw, and I queried them
about how he would feel if she spent time with her female
friends after they were married, and he with his male
friends, and other things. I probed because I was scratch-
ing for unhealthy jealousy: "You're mine! You be home
every night! You give everything to me!" Now, that would
be unhealthy jealousy.

There is, however, a very healthy jealousy. If Noël
decides she's interested in another man, if she starts
hanging out for long hours at Starbucks with him, having
deep conversations about her heart, and gets further and
further from my heart, I should be really angry. And God
is really angry when we hang out in inappropriate ways
with the world. Why? Because we're designed to bestow

all the glory on him, to get our deepest and most profound satisfaction from him. He is intending to say in the law, "I'm number one—period. And you'll be destroyed if you don't agree." Now that kind of talk really turns people off. But you need to say it like that just to wake some people up to how carnal and self-centered they are. That's the law.

Mercy in the Wilderness

The Israelites wandered in the wilderness a long time. Why? Why did he spare them? These were really, really rebellious folks, just like we are apart from God.

> But the house of Israel rebelled against me in the wilderness. They did not walk in my statutes but rejected my rules, by which, if a person does them, he shall live; and my Sabbaths they greatly profaned. Then I said I would pour out my wrath upon them in the wilderness, to make a full end of them. But I acted for the sake of my name, that it should not be profaned in the sight of the nations, in whose sight I had brought them out. (Ezekiel 20:13–14)

We've seen that before. It happens over and over again in the history of Israel.

Gospel before the Gospel

We will skip the conquest of Canaan and move to the Israelites asking for a king. I love this passage because it is so full of gospel before the gospel. We saw the gospel in the exodus, that the salvation of a rebellious people was rooted not in their worth, but in God's worth. And here we're going to see it again. The people have asked to have a king like the nations, and Samuel's not happy about that, and God's angry about that. So, what happens?

> And all the people said to Samuel, "Pray for your servants to the LORD your God, that we may not die, for we have added to all our sins this evil, to ask for ourselves a king." And Samuel said to the people, "Do not be afraid; you have done all this evil." (1 Samuel 12:19–20)

I don't remember how many years ago it was, but there was a point where I read this and I thought, that is a very strange connection. The connection between "fear not" and "you have done all this evil" is really weird. It should be, "Fear! You have done all this evil. Fear!" But it says, "Fear not; you have done all this evil." That's what I mean by *gospel*. This is undeserved grace, undeserved mercy. Why? What's the basis of it?

> Do not be afraid; you have done all this evil. Yet do not turn aside from following the LORD, but serve the LORD with all your heart. And do not turn aside after empty things that cannot profit or deliver, for they are empty. For the LORD will not forsake his people, for his great name's sake. (1 Samuel 12:20–22)

So in the exodus, the people were delivered and not shown wrath because God was jealous for his name in Egypt. Here, the people have committed treason and impeached God and essentially said, "We want another kind of king. We want to be like the nations. We don't like this theoc-

racy business. We want another king." Later, they called
it sin, and Samuel preached to them and told them not to
be afraid. Samuel could have said, "Don't be afraid because
God is merciful, God is gracious, God keeps covenant
love." He could have said all these things and they would
be true, but instead, he said, "The Lord will not cast away
his people for his great name's sake."

How Do You Pray?

How do you pray in response to that?

I remember being at Fuller Seminary in the spring
of 1969, when my world was being blown to smithereens.
I went through Copernican revolutions, because when
you've been man-centered all your life, all the stars must
come crashing down in order to rebuild your world. Noël
and I had just gotten married in December of 1968, so she
was walking through this with me.

Every night as a young couple, we knelt by the beige
couch in the living room of that little house on Orange
Grove Boulevard and prayed. I remember saying to Noël,
"You know, you can tell when somebody's theology is being
turned upside down by the way they pray." Because we
just were praying differently. Texts like "Hallowed be thy
name" were just exploding. That wasn't a throwaway phrase
anymore! "Hallowed be your name" was a request to God
to make himself strong in the world and great in our
hearts. So I'm asking you: how does your discovery of God
affect your praying?

Here's one way: "*For thy name's sake*, O LORD, pardon
my guilt, for it is great" (Psalm 25:11). Do you pray that
way? Does that kind of thinking come to your mind? It

sure didn't come to my mind until I had my eyes open to texts, hundreds of them, like that.

We do say this now, just in different words. We say, "In Jesus's name I pray, amen." Because on this side of the cross, we know *the name*—it's Jesus. God has put his Son forward to exalt his own righteousness and preserve his own justice in the saving of sinners. So when we call down mercy, totally undeserved, whom are we going to appeal to? Ourselves? Nothing works except this: "For your name's sake, O Lord, make your name great in forgiving my sins and using me, broken and imperfect as I am."

Or how about this prayer: "He leads me in paths of righteousness for his name's sake" (Psalm 23:3). Why does he sanctify you, leading you in paths of righteousness? Well consider how you might pray in response to that verse. "Lord, lead me in paths of righteousness *for your name's sake* today—I want you to *look great* today."

Brokenness before Joy

Noël and I had a rocking chair that I bought for her when we had our first baby in Germany. I sat in that chair every Sunday night. There were no Sunday-evening events in Germany, and for about a year I read *Religious Affections* by Jonathan Edwards. I read two or three pages a night—I could not take much of that book. It was absolutely convicting.

Ezekiel 36 jumped off the page in Edwards's section on what he called evangelical humiliation.

Therefore say to the house of Israel, Thus says the Lord GOD: It is not for your sake, O house of

Israel, that I am about to act, but for the sake of
my holy name, which you have profaned among
the nations to which you came. And I will vindicate the holiness of my great name, which has
been profaned among the nations, and which you
have profaned among them. And the nations will
know that I am the Lord, declares the Lord God,
when through you I vindicate my holiness before
their eyes .... It is not for your sake that I will act,
declares the Lord God; let that be known to you.
Be ashamed and confounded for your ways, O
house of Israel. (Ezekiel 36:22–23, 32)

The reason that blew me away in 1972 is because I was
surrounded by books on self-esteem. And as I read Ezekiel
36, I thought, *None of those books would ever quote this text.
They would never, ever, ever say, "It is not for your sake I will
act, says the Lord; let that be known to you. Be ashamed and
confounded for your sins, O house of Israel."*

We must feel genuine, devastating brokenness before
we leap for joy at the cross. The cross first says, "It is
because of you that I am here. Your sin is so horrible it
requires the death of the Son of God for God to be vindicated in the saving of your soul."

Jesus Glorifies the Father

We see the same thing in the New Testament. Jesus says, "I
glorified you on earth, having accomplished the work that
you gave me to do" (John 17:4).

In accomplishing the work that Jesus received from
the Father, he was glorifying the Father. And in John 7:18

Jesus says, "The one who speaks on his own authority seeks his own glory; but the one who seeks the glory of him who sent him is true, and in him there is no falsehood." God sent Jesus to get glory for God! That's why he sent him.

In Romans 15:8–9, Paul says, "For I tell you that Christ became a servant to the circumcised to show God's truthfulness, in order to confirm the promises given to the patriarchs, and in order that the Gentiles might glorify God for his mercy."

The reason God sent Jesus was so the Gentiles would glorify God for his mercy.

What does that little preposition *for* mean there: "glorify God *for* his mercy"? Wouldn't you paraphrase that, "glorify God *on the basis of* his mercy"? That is, the experience of mercy prompts the glorifying of God *for* the mercy. God gets the glory, we get the mercy, and that's the best of all possible worlds. I wouldn't want it any other way. The natural mind says, "No, I really can't be happy unless I get the glory, and I don't like a God who doesn't need a little bit of mercy." I sometimes hear people talk about "forgiving God." I've got to watch my language when I hear things like that.

How God Justifies Sinners

Romans contains the most important paragraph in the Bible, probably. It's dangerous to say things like that, but if I had to choose, it would be somewhere in Romans 8 or somewhere in Romans 3.

In Romans 3, Paul sets up the issue of human sin in terms of glory: "All have sinned and fall short of the glory of God" (Romans 3:23). Back in Romans 1, we read that we have all exchanged the glory of God for images, especially the one in the mirror. Romans 1:23 says, "[We] exchanged the glory of the immortal God for images resembling mortal man and birds and animals and creeping things."

Then in Romans 3:23, Paul says, "All have sinned and *fall short*," which literally means *lack*. We lack because we have traded the glory of God for lesser things. We have turned away from it and embraced our favorite glory. *All have sinned*, and that's what sin is. Preferring another glory to God's glory is what sin is. *All have sinned and fall short of the glory of God.*

Now here is how God justifies sinners:

> All have sinned and fall short of the glory of God, and are justified by his grace as a gift, through the redemption that is in Christ Jesus, whom God put forward as a propitiation by his blood, to be received by faith. This was to show God's righteousness, because in his divine forbearance he had passed over former sins. It was to show his righteousness at the present time, so that he might be just and the justifier of the one who has faith in Jesus. (Romans 3:23–26)

If God passes over sins in the Old Testament and in your life—if he just passes them over—what does it look like? Sins belittle the glory of God, making his glory of little value. How then can God be righteous and forgive you? And the answer is that he killed his Son to show how serious sin is. He bruised his Son in order to magnify the worth of his glory.

Everything in redemptive history has been God acting for his glory; therefore, everything in your life is to join him in that purpose. The reason you're on the planet is to join God in making much of God. Every human being that you'll ever meet, anywhere in the world, in any culture, according to Romans 5, is disobedient and rebellious and needs to be justified by faith alone. They've all stopped glorifying God for who he really is, and we go to call them back to glorify God.

Why Is Jesus Coming Back?

Let's jump all the way to the end now, to the second coming. Why is Jesus coming back?

> They will suffer the punishment of eternal destruction, away from the presence of the Lord and from the glory of his might, when he comes on that day to be glorified in his saints, and to be marveled at among all who have believed, because our testimony to you was believed. (2 Thessalonians 1:9–10)

Second Thessalonians 1 gives us two reasons why the Son of God is returning to earth: to be glorified and to be marveled at. I never thought that for the first twenty-two years of my life. If anybody had asked me why Jesus is coming back, I'd have said, "He's coming back to get me—to save me." And that's true; it's just skewed. I was ignorant. My mind was not his mind. My thoughts were not his thoughts. They weren't based on what God's thoughts are based on. The Son of God is coming to be glorified, and the reason this is love is because your joy at that moment will consist in making much of him!

Admiring the Most Admirable

Ayn Rand, the atheistic philosopher novelist, said in *Atlas Shrugged*: "Admiration is the rarest of pleasures." Now, in her mouth, that was absolutely scornful, meaning, "There aren't any admirable people in the world except me and a few philosopher-business types." But in my mouth it means that, unlike all other creatures, as a human, I am made to be one who admires. And my deepest joy will consist in admiring the most admirable. And there is only one who is most admirable: Christ, the complete image of God. And when he comes, my fullest joy will consist in fulfilling the purpose for which he came—namely, to be admired. So his glory and my joy come together.

Now, if you embrace this, then you will know why Jesus came to purchase people from every ethnic group, and why the church sends out missionaries. It's all *for the sake of God's name.* If we want our heart for the nations to rest upon God's heart for the nations, it should rest upon the *basis* of God's heart for the nations—namely, God's heart for his own glory.

COLOSSIANS 1:24-26

Now I rejoice in my sufferings for your sake, and in my flesh I am filling up what is lacking in Christ's afflictions for the sake of his body, that is, the church, [25] of which I became a minister according to the stewardship from God that was given to me for you, to make the word of God fully known, [26] the mystery hidden for ages and generations but now revealed to his saints.

2

Doing Missions
When Dying
Is Gain

My mission statement in life—and the mission statement of
the church I served for thirty three years, from 1980 to 2013—
is "we exist to spread a passion for the supremacy of God in
all things for the joy of all peoples through Jesus Christ."

I love that mission statement for several reasons.
One is because I know it cannot fail. I know it cannot
fail because it's a promise from Jesus. "This gospel of the
kingdom will be proclaimed throughout the whole world
as a testimony to all the nations, and then the end will
come" (Matthew 24:14). *Nations* in that verse does not refer
to political states. It refers to something like what we call
people groups, ethnolinguistic groupings, and we may be
absolutely certain that every one of them will be penetrated by the gospel, and they will be gathered with God's
global people in the new heavens and new earth.

The Promise Is Sure

Let me give you four reasons why we can bank on that.

1. Jesus never lies.

> *Heaven and earth will pass away, but my words*
> *will not pass away. (Matthew 24:35)*

Because Jesus spoke these words, this mission called *world evangelization* is going to be completed. It's going to be done, and you can either get on board and enjoy the triumph, or you can cop out and waste your life. You have only those two choices, because there is no middle option like, "Maybe it won't succeed, and I can be on the best side by not jumping on board." That won't happen.

2. The ransom has already been paid for God's people among all the nations.

> *Worthy are you to take the scroll and to open its seals,*
> *for you were slain, and by your blood you ransomed*
> *people for God from every tribe and language and*
> *people and nation, and you have made them a*
> *kingdom and priests to our God, and they shall reign*
> *on the earth. (Revelation 5:9–10)*

These people have been ransomed, paid for, and God will not go back on his Son's payment.

I love the story of the Moravians. In northern Germany, two of them were getting on a boat, ready to sell themselves into slavery in the West Indies, if necessary, never to come back again. And as the boat drifts out into the harbor they lift their hands and say, "May the Lamb receive the reward of his suffering." What they meant was that Christ had already bought those people. And they were going to find them. They would go preaching the gospel to everyone they could, and trusting God to call the ransomed to himself.

We know God's global mission can't abort because the debt has been paid for each of God's people everywhere in the world. Those lost sheep, as Jesus called them, that are scattered throughout the world, will come in as the Father calls them through the preaching of the gospel (John 11:51–52).

3. The glory of God is at stake.

Christ became a servant to the circumcised to show God's truthfulness, in order to confirm the promises given to the patriarchs, and in order that the Gentiles might glorify God for his mercy. (Romans 15:8–9).

The whole purpose of the incarnation was to bring glory to the Father through the manifestation of his mercy to the nations.

The glory of God is at stake in the Great Commission. In 1983 at Bethlehem Baptist Church, Tom Steller—my partner in ministry for thirty-three years at the church—and I were both met by God in amazing ways. Tom, in the middle of the night, couldn't sleep, so he got up, put on a John Michael Talbot album, lay down on the couch, and heard our theology translated into missions. We had been a glory-of-God-oriented leadership, but we had not yet made sense of missions like we ought. John Michael Talbot was singing about the glory of God filling the earth the way the waters cover the sea, and Tom wept for an hour.

At the same time, God was moving on my wife, Noël,

and me to ask, "What can we do to make our church a launching pad for missions?" Everything came together to make an electric moment in the life of our church, and it all flowed from a passion for the glory of God.

4. God is sovereign.

> *Let us leave the elementary doctrine of Christ and go on to maturity. . . . And this we will do if God permits. (Hebrews 6:1, 3)*

In the late 1990s, as I was preaching sequentially through Hebrews, we arrived at Hebrews 6—a very difficult text about whether people who fall away are genuine Christians or not. In verses 1–3, there is this amazing statement (just a tiny piece of the massive biblical evidence for why I'm a Calvinist).

When we looked at this together, there fell across my congregation the most amazing silence. We heard the implications of the words *if God permits*. Naturally, they asked, "You mean God might *not* permit a body of believers to go on to maturity?"

God is sovereign. He is sovereign in the church, and he is sovereign among the nations. One testimony to this is in that memorable article in *Christianity Today* years ago retelling the story of Jim Elliot, Nate Saint, Pete Flemming, Roger Youderian, and Ed McCully. Steve Saint, Nate's son, tells the story of his dad getting speared by Waodanis in Ecuador. He tells it after having learned new details of intrigue in the Waodani tribe that were responsible for this killing. These new details implied that the killings were very unlikely. They simply should not have happened; it made no sense. Yet it did happen.

Having discovered the intrigue, he wrote this article. There was one sentence that absolutely blew me out of my living room chair. He wrote, "As [the natives] described their recollections, it occurred to me how incredibly unlikely it was that the palm beach killing took place at all. It is an anomaly that I cannot explain outside of divine intervention."[1]

Don't miss that. He says, "I can explain the spearing of my dad only by virtue of divine intervention." Do you hear what this son is saying? "God killed my dad." He believes that, and I believe that. In Revelation 6:10, martyrs who shed their blood for the gospel are saying, "O Sovereign Lord, holy and true, how long before you will judge and avenge our blood?" The answer comes back, "Then they were each given a white robe and told to rest a little longer, until the number of their fellow servants and their brothers should be complete, who were to be killed as they themselves had been" (Revelation 6:11). God says, "Rest until the number that I have appointed is complete." He has in mind a certain number of martyrs. When it is complete, then the end will come.

God is sovereign over the best and worst that happens in world missions. Therefore, the mission cannot fail.

The Price Is Suffering

The price of God's global mission is suffering, and the volatility in the world today against the church is not decreasing. It is increasing, especially among the groups that need the gospel most. There is no such thing as a

1. https://www.christianitytoday.com/ct/1996/september16/missionaries-did-they-have-to-die.html

"closed country." That notion has no root or warrant in the Bible, and it would have been unintelligible to the apostle Paul, who laid down his life in every city he visited.

One Sunday, along with many other churches across the nation, our church was focusing on the suffering church. We saw videos or heard stories about places like Sudan, where the Muslim regime was systematically ostracizing and starving Christians, so that there were about five hundred martyrs a day in Sudan. In light of this, I got very tired of candidates for staff positions in our inner-city church asking, "Will our children be safe?" I've grown tired of such American priorities infecting the mission of the church. Whoever said that your children would be safe in the call of God?

Youth with a Mission (YWAM) is a wild-eyed, radical group that I love. I got an email from them some years ago saying,

> One hundred and fifty men armed with
> machetes surrounded the premises occupied by
> the YWAM team in India. The mob had been
> incited by other religious groups in an effort to
> chase them off. As the mob pressed in, someone
> in a key moment spoke up on the team's behalf,
> and they decided to give them thirty days to
> leave. The team feels they should not leave
> and that their ministry work in the city is at
> stake. Much fruit has been seen in a previously
> unreached region, and there is great potential for
> more. In the past when violence has broken out
> between rival religious groups, people have lost
> their lives. Please pray for them to have wisdom.

This is exactly the opposite of what I hear, mainly in America, as people decide where to live, for example. I don't hear people saying, "I don't want to leave, because this is where I'm called to and this is where there's need." Oh that we might see a reversal of our self-centered priorities! They seem to be woven into the very fabric of our consumer culture: move toward comfort, toward security, toward ease, toward safety, away from stress, away from trouble, and away from danger. It ought to be exactly the opposite. It was Jesus himself who said, "If anyone would come after me, let him deny himself and take up his cross and follow me" (Matthew 16:24).

We have absorbed a culture of consumerism, comfort, and ease in the church. It creates weak ministries and churches in which safe, secure, nice things are done for each other, and safe excursions are made to help save some others. But oh, we won't *live* there, and we won't *stay* there—not even in America, not to mention Saudi Arabia.

I was in Amsterdam once talking to another wild-eyed, wonderful missions group, Frontiers, founded by one of my heroes, Greg Livingstone. In front of me sat five hundred people who were risking their lives every day among Muslim peoples. During the conference they were getting emails, which they would stand up and read. They would say, "Please pray for X. He was stabbed in the chest three times yesterday, and the worst thing is his children were watching him. He's in the hospital in critical condition." Then we would go to prayer. The next day, another email would come, and this time six Christian brothers in Morocco had been arrested. And so we prayed. Updates like these continued to come in throughout the conference. And at the end of it, the missionaries were ready to go back.

Am I going to come back to America and be the same? Will I stand up in front of my church and say, "Let's have nice, comfortable, easy services. Let's just be comfortable and secure"? Golgotha is not a suburb of Jerusalem. Let us go with him outside the camp and suffer with him and bear reproach (Hebrews 13:13).

Suffering Is Also the Means

But in saying there will be martyrs and there must be suffering, I haven't yet said the main thing about the price of getting the job done. That's because suffering is not just the price of missions but also the means.

Consider Colossians 1:24: "Now I rejoice in my sufferings," Paul says. He was a very strange person. "I rejoice in my sufferings" is very counter-cultural, very un-American—indeed, very counter-human. "I rejoice in my sufferings for your sake, and in my flesh I am filling up what is lacking in Christ's afflictions for the sake of his body, that is, the church."

That's on the brink of blasphemy. What does he mean by "filling up what is lacking" in the afflictions of our great God and Savior, Jesus Christ? How could *his* afflictions be lacking? Paul does not mean that in his own sufferings he improves upon the merit and the atoning worth of Jesus's blood. That's not what he means. Well then, what does he mean?

Personal Presentation

There is a remarkable parallel to Colossians 1:24 in Philippians 2:30. What makes it a parallel is the coming together of the same two words, one for *fill up* (or *complete*) and the other for *what is lacking*. Paul says that Epaphroditus "nearly died for the work of Christ, risking his life to *complete what was lacking* in your service to me."

Epaphroditus was sent from the Philippian church over to Paul in Rome. He risked his life to get there, and Paul extols him for risking his life. He tells the Philippians that they should receive such a one with honor, because he was sick unto death and risked his neck to complete their ministry to him.

I opened up my hundred-year-old commentary on Philippians by Martin Vincent and read an explanation of that verse that I think is a perfect interpretation of Colossians 1:24. Vincent says,

> The gift to Paul from the Philippians was a gift of the church as a body. It was a sacrificial offering of love. What was lacking was the church's presentation of this offering in person. This was impossible, and Paul represents Epaphroditus as supplying this lack by his affectionate, zealous ministry.[2]

So the picture is of a church that wants to communicate love in the form of money to Paul in Rome, and they can't do it. There's too many of them to go and show their love as group, and it's too far away. So they say, in essence, "Epaphroditus, represent us and *complete what is lacking in our love*. There's nothing lacking in our love except the *expression* of our love in person there. Take it and communicate it to Paul."

---

2. Marvin R. Vincent, *Philippians and Philemon* (1897; repr., New York: T&T Clark, 2000), 75.

Now that's exactly what I think Colossians 1:24 means. Jesus dies and he suffers for people all over the world in every nation. Then he is buried, and raised on the third day, according to the Scriptures. Then he ascends into heaven where he reigns over the world. And he leaves a work to be done.

Paul's understanding of his own mission is that there is one thing lacking in the sufferings of Jesus: *the love offering of Christ is to be presented in person through missionaries to the peoples for whom he died.* And Paul says he does this through his sufferings: "In my flesh I am filling up what is lacking in Christ's afflictions." This means that Christ intends for the Great Commission to be a presentation to the nations of the sufferings of his cross through the sufferings of his people. That's the way it will be finished. If you sign up for the Great Commission, that's what you sign up for.

"We Saw Your Blistered Feet"

In the early '90s, when I was working on the book *Let the Nations Be Glad*, I hid away at Trinity Seminary in Deerfield, Illinois, on a writing leave. Then I got word that J. Oswald Sanders—an 89-year-old veteran missions leader—was going to be in chapel. I wanted to hear him, so I snuck into the back of chapel and listened to him. And this 89-year-old man stood up there, and I was just oozing with admiration and desire to be like him when I'm 89. He told a story that embodies Colossians 1:24.

He said there was once an evangelist in India who trudged on foot to various villages preaching the gospel. This evangelist was a simple man with no education, who loved Jesus with all his heart and was ready to lay down his life. He came to a village that didn't have the gospel. It was late in the day, and he was very tired. But he went into the village and lifted his voice and shared the gospel with those gathered in the square. They mocked him, derided him, and drove him out of town. And he was so tired— with no emotional resources left—that he lay down under a tree, utterly discouraged. He went to sleep not knowing if he would ever wake up. They might come kill him, for all he knew.

Suddenly, just after dusk, he was startled and woke up. The whole town seemed to be around him, looking at him. He thought he would probably die. One of the big men in the village said, "We came out to see what kind of man you are, and when we saw your blistered feet, we knew you were a holy man. We want you to tell us why you were willing to get blistered feet to come talk to us." So he preached the gospel and, according to Sanders, the whole village believed. I think that's what Paul means by, "In my flesh I am filling up what is lacking in Christ's afflictions."

In Ministry Past 70

I have one other small parenthesis about J. Oswald Sanders. At 89 years old, he said, "I've written a book a year since I was 70." Eighteen books after 70! There are people in my church and all over America abandoning productive life at 65 and dying on the golf course, when they ought to be laying their lives down among the Muslims, like Raymond Lull, who was a twelfth-century oriental scholar and Muslim missionary. As he grew old, he thought, "What am I doing? I'm going to die here in Italy. Why not die preaching the gospel in Algeria?" And so, knowing that's what it would cost him to preach publicly, he got on a boat

at 80-something years of age and crossed the Mediter-
ranean. He stayed underground a while, encouraging the
church, and then he decided it was as good a time as any.
So he stood up and preached, and they killed him. What a
way to go!

Why should we think that putting in our forty or fifty
years on the job should mean that we should play games
for the last fifteen years before we meet the King? This is
biblically incomprehensible. We're strong at 65, and we're
strong at 70.

My father, who died in 2007, was bursting with
ministry in his late seventies and early eighties. I can
remember twenty-five years before that, when my mother
was killed, and he was almost killed, in a bus accident in
Israel. I picked him up at the Atlanta airport along with
my mother's body ten days after the accident. In the
ambulance, all the way home from Atlanta to Greenville,
South Carolina, he lay there with his back completely
lacerated, and he kept saying, "God must have a purpose
for me. God must have a purpose for me!" He could not
fathom that his wife of thirty-six years was gone and God
had spared him.

Indeed, God did have a purpose for him. It wasn't
long before his life exploded with new ministry, especially
globally. He was working harder in his seventies for the
nations than ever before. He prepared lessons from Easley,
South Carolina, including some tapes, and they were in
sixty nations, with about ten thousand people believing in
Jesus every year, because God spared my dad and caused
him not to believe in retirement.

The Prize Is Satisfying

How do you love like that? Where are you going to get this kind of courage and motivation? Are you feeling ready for this? Do you think you have it within you to be able to endure this?

Read Stephen Neill's *A History of Christian Missions*. He describes what happened in Japan when the gospel came there in the 1500s. The emperor began to believe that the incursion of the Christian faith into their religious sphere was so threatening that they must end it. And he did end it, with absolutely incredible brutality. It was over for the church in Japan. And I don't doubt that the hardness and difficulty of Japan today is largely owing to the massive (though short-term) triumph of the devil in the early 1600s.

> Twenty-seven Jesuits, fifteen friars, and five secular clergy did manage to evade the order of banishment. It was not until April 1617 that the first martyrdoms of Europeans took place, a Jesuit and a Franciscan being beheaded at Omura at that time, and a Dominican and an Augustinian a little later in the same area. Every kind of cruelty was practiced on the pitiable victims of the persecution. Crucifixion was the method usually employed in the case of Japanese Christians. On one occasion seventy Japanese at Yedo were crucified upside down at low water and were drowned as the tide came in.[3]

I cried when I first read that, because I have a good

---

3. Stephen Neill, *A History of Christian Missions*, 2nd ed. (New York: Penguin, 1986), 137.

enough imagination to picture the lapping water with your wife on one side and your 16-year-old on the other.

Are you ready? Do you think you've got that within you? You don't. No way does anybody have that kind of resourcefulness within him. Where are we going to get it? That's what I want to close with.

Plundered and Rejoicing

We're going to get it by believing the promises of God. Hebrews 10:32–33 is my favorite text about where we get the resources to live like this: "Recall the former days when, after you were enlightened, you endured a hard struggle with sufferings, sometimes being publicly exposed to reproach and affliction, and sometimes being partners with those so treated."

Now let me stop there and give you the situation. In the early days of the church, persecution arose. Some of them suffered outright and publicly, and others had compassion on those who were suffering. You'll see in verse 34 that some of those in the church were imprisoned, and others went to visit them.

Those who were in prison in those days probably depended on others for food and water and any kind of physical care that they would need. But that meant that their friends and neighbors had to go public and identify with them. That's risky business when someone's been put in jail because they're a Christian. So those who were still free went underground for a few hours (I'm imagining this) and asked, "What are we going to do?" And somebody said "Psalm 63:3 tells us that the steadfast love of the Lord is better than life. It's *better than life*. Let's go!" And if Martin Luther would have been there, he would have said,

"Let goods and kindred go, this mortal life also. The body they may kill; God's truth abideth still. His kingdom is forever. Let's go!" And that's exactly what they did.

Here's the rest of the text: "You had compassion on those in prison, and you joyfully accepted the plundering of your property" (Hebrews 10:34). Now here's what happened. They had compassion on the prisoners, which means they went to them. And their property—house, chariot, horses, mules, carpentry tools, chairs, whatever—was set on fire by a mob, or maybe just ransacked and thrown to the streets by people with machetes. And when they looked over their shoulder to see what was happening back there, they *rejoiced*.

What do you do when somebody bashes your computer while you're trying to minister to them? Or when you drive downtown to serve the poor, and they smash your windshield, get your radio, or slash your tires? If you're not like these radical Christians in Hebrews 10:34, you're probably not going to be a very good candidate for martyrdom either. So the question is, How are we going to be like this? I want to be like this. That's why I love this text.

I make no claim to be a perfect embodiment of this. But I want to be like this, so that when a rock comes sailing through my kitchen window—like it has done multiple times over the years—and smashes the glass and my wife and children hit the floor not knowing if it's a bullet or a grenade, I want to be able to say, "Isn't this a great neighborhood to live in? This is where the needs are. You see those five teenage kids that just rode by? They need Jesus. If we move out of here, who's going to tell them about Jesus?"

God's Precious Promises

Finally, to the main point of the text: how did they have
the wherewithal to rejoice at the plundering of their
property and the risking of their lives? Here's the answer:
"Since you knew that you yourselves had a better possession
and an abiding one." Their love and their courage came
from knowing they had a great reward beyond the grave. It
was that real to them.

If you are a Christian, God is holding out to you
indescribably wonderful promises. "'I will never leave you
nor forsake you.' So we can confidently say, 'The Lord
is my helper; I will not fear; what can man do to me?'"
(Hebrews 13:5–6). What can man do to you? Well, actually,
man can kill you. But that is no final defeat, because we
know what Romans 8:35–39 says.

> Who shall separate us from the love of Christ?
> Shall tribulation, or distress, or persecution, or
> famine, or nakedness, or danger, or sword? As
> it is written, 'For your sake we are being killed
> all the day long; we are regarded as sheep to be
> slaughtered.' No, in all these things we are more
> than conquerors through him who loved us. For
> I am sure that neither death nor life, nor angels
> nor rulers, nor things present nor things to come,
> nor powers, nor height nor depth, nor anything
> else in all creation, will be able to separate us
> from the love of God in Christ Jesus our Lord.

Therefore, nothing can ultimately harm you.

Do you remember what Jesus said in Luke 21:16–18?
"Some of you they will put to death .... But not a hair of
your head will perish." What does that mean? It's Romans

8:28. Everything, including death, works together for your good. When you die, you don't perish. To die is gain. Doing missions when death is gain is the greatest life in the world.

JOHN 10:16

I have other sheep that are not of this fold. I must bring them also, and they will listen to my voice. So there will be one flock, one shepherd.

3

The Voice of the Sovereign Shepherd

One of the most moving books I have read about the history of modern missions is *The St. Andrews Seven* by Stuart Piggin and John Roxborogh.[4] It tells the story of how the life and teaching of Thomas Chalmers at the University of St. Andrews inspired six of his best students in the 1820s to radical missionary commitment, resulting in 141 years of combined service on the mission field.

I mention this book because it gives a historical illustration of the truth that a vision for missions flows down from a vision of the greatness of God and his grand design for the world. The missionary zeal of these six students came from the glorious sight of God they received from Chalmers.

---

4. Stuart Piggin and John Roxborogh, *The St. Andrews Seven* (Carlisle, PA: Banner of Truth, 1985).

The Sight That Sustains Missions

That group of students was part of the second generation of modern missions. The first generation illustrates the same principle. Consider, for example, William Carey, the father of modern missions, who gave forty years of his life in India and never went home on furlough.

In 1797, four years after Carey came to India, he was confronted by a Brahman. When Carey had preached on Acts 14:16 and 17:30, he said that God formerly allowed all men everywhere to go their own way, but now he commands all men everywhere to repent. The Brahman responded, "Indeed I think God ought to repent for not sending the gospel sooner to us."

Here was a crucial need for deep biblical doctrine. The Brahman's objection is not easy to answer. Listen to how Carey responded and see if you would have thought of such an answer.

> To this I added, suppose a kingdom had been long overrun by the enemies of its true king, and he, though possessed of sufficient power to conquer them, should yet suffer them to prevail, and establish themselves as much as they could desire, would not the valor and wisdom of that king be far more conspicuous in exterminating them, than it would have been if he had opposed them at first, and prevented their entering the country? Thus by the diffusion of gospel light, the wisdom, power, and grace of God will be more conspicuous in overcoming such deep-rooted idolatries, and in destroying all that darkness and vice which have so universally

> prevailed in this country, than they would have
> been if all had not been suffered to walk in their
> own ways for so many ages past.[5]

What an answer! The sovereign God rules the nations in such a way that even the ages of unbelief will redound to his glory when the gospel victory comes. Carey did not say that God was unable to get the gospel to India sooner because of his stubborn and disobedient people. Carey knew that such impotence is simply not worthy of the name of God.

The origin of modern missions sprang up among pastors in England who were decidedly doctrinal in their life and preaching. Andrew Fuller, Samuel Pearce, John Sutcliffe, and William Carey were all of this sort. This was the little band of brothers from which such amazing missionary endeavors sprung in the late 1700s.

Their majestic view of God moved them to lay claim to the nations on behalf of the risen Christ, who said, "All authority in heaven and on earth has been given to me. Go therefore and make disciples of all nations" (Matthew 28:18–19). The modern missionary movement was born in this majestic view of the sovereignty of God and the global authority of Jesus Christ.

My aim in this chapter is to show how the majesty and the glory of God, and his absolute authority and power, awaken and sustain a passion for world missions. This vision of God is what fuels the mission to reach all the ethnolinguistic people groups of the world with the good news that the Son of God, Jesus Christ, has come and died in our place to remove the guilt and condemna-

---

5. Tom Wells, *A Vision for Missions* (Carlisle, PA: Banner of Truth, 1985), 13.

tion of sin and has risen from the dead to destroy death and secure everlasting life and joy for all who will believe in his name.

Six Observations from John 10

In John 10:16, one of the great missionary texts in the Gospel of John, Jesus says, "I have other sheep that are not of this fold. I must bring them also, and they will listen to my voice. So there will be one flock, one shepherd." In order to understand this missionary promise of Christ, we need to notice at least six things in the context of John 10.

1. Jesus calls himself a shepherd.

> *I am the good shepherd. (John 10:11, 14)*

The flock of God is the people of Israel. We know this because later, in verse 16, Jesus refers to "other sheep that are not of this fold"—namely, Gentile converts. This leads to the second observation.

2. Some sheep are Christ's, and some are not.

> *[The shepherd] calls his own sheep by name and leads them out. When he has brought out all his own, he goes before them. (John 10:3–4)*

> *I am the good shepherd; I know my own and my own know me. (John 10:14)*

In other words, not all the people in the flock of Israel truly belonged to Christ. Some were his sheep; some weren't.

3. God the Father gave these sheep to the Son.

My Father, who has given them to me, is greater than all, and no one is able to snatch them out of the Father's hand. (John 10:29)

This is Jesus's way of talking about the doctrine of election. God the Father has chosen a people for his own. These are his sheep. He then gives them to his Son so that they can be saved by faith in him. You can see this clearly in John 17:6, where Jesus says to his Father, "I have manifested your name to the people whom you gave me out of the world. Yours they were, and you gave them to me, and they have kept your word." And you can see it in John 6:37, where Jesus says, "All that the Father gives me will come to me, and whoever comes to me I will never cast out."

So Jesus can speak with confidence about some sheep among the flock of Israel that are definitely his, because they first belonged to the Father before they ever came to Jesus or believed in Jesus. The Father had chosen them for himself—"yours they were"—and then he had given them to the Son—"and you gave them to me" (see also John 6:39, 44, 65; 17:9, 24; 18:9).

4. Because Jesus's sheep are already his, they hear his voice.

The sheep hear his voice, and he calls his own sheep by name and leads them out. When he has brought out all his own, he goes before them, and the sheep follow him, for they know his voice. (John 10:3–4)

> *My sheep hear my voice, and I know them, and they*
> *follow me. (John 10:27)*

Do you see the thrust of these verses? Being one of
Christ's sheep *enables* you to respond to his call. It is not
the other way around in these verses: responding to his
call does not make you one of his sheep. If you hear and
recognize his voice, it is because you are *already* one of his
sheep, chosen by the Father. You come to the Son because
the Father gave you to the Son (John 6:44, 65; 17:6).

That is the startling thing about this chapter. And it
can be very offensive to a self-sufficient, unbelieving heart.
It reveals to us the presumption of ultimate self-determi-
nation—of thinking that the final, decisive determination
of our salvation lies in our own power. Listen carefully to
verse 26: "You do not believe because you are not among
my sheep."

The final boast of unbelief is destroyed by the doctrine
of election. Those whom God chose he also gave to the
Son, and those whom he gave to the Son, the Son also
called by name, and those whom the Son called hear his
voice and believe.

5. Jesus lays down his life for his sheep.

> *I am the good shepherd. The good shepherd lays down*
> *his life for the sheep. (John 10:11)*

> *I am the good shepherd. I know my own and my*
> *own know me, just as the Father knows me and I*
> *know the Father; and I lay down my life for the*
> *sheep. (John 10:14–15)*

To echo the words of Paul in Romans 8:30, those whom

the Father has made his own he also gave to the Son, and those whom he gave to the Son, the Son also called, and those whom the Son called he also justified, by laying down his life for the sheep.

6. Jesus gives eternal life to his sheep.

My sheep hear my voice, and I know them, and they follow me. I give them eternal life, and they will never perish, and no one will snatch them out of my hand. My Father, who has given them to me, is greater than all, and no one is able to snatch them out of the Father's hand. I and the Father are one. (John 10:27–30)

Jesus not only lays his life down for the sheep. He also gives them eternal life that no one can ever take away.

So the picture we have in John 10 is of a great Shepherd who sovereignly saves his sheep.

- The Father gives them to him.
- He dies for them.
- He calls them by name.
- He gives them eternal life.
- And he keeps them safe forever.

What a great salvation we have! What a great Savior!

Sheep Beyond the Fold

And now a great danger arises for us. Satan takes every great truth and throws up a plausible distortion of it. He did that in William Carey's day. Some Christians had taken this pride-shattering doctrine of salvation through sovereign grace and twisted it into an in-house, elitist doctrine for the private comfort of the chosen few, with no burden to reach the nations of the world.

But God in his mercy has again and again made clear to his servants that his salvation is not the prerogative of any one group on earth. Just when the Jewish disciples began to feel like they were the real, select heirs of Abraham, Jesus strikes in John 10:16: "I have other sheep that are not of this fold," sheep from among the Gentiles.

Just when the early American Puritans were settling into their "chosen" status as the New Israel in the New England, Jesus said to John Eliot, "I have other sheep that are not of this Puritan fold—among the Algonquin Indians." And Jesus said one hundred years later to David Brainerd, "I have other sheep that are not of this Congregational fold—among the Susquehanna."

Just when the Particular Baptists of England were being frozen in the unbiblical ice of hyper-Calvinism, Jesus spoke to William Carey: "I have other sheep that are not of this English fold—in India."

Just when the mission agencies and churches were growing content with the coastland successes around the world, Jesus stirred up Hudson Taylor and said, "I have other sheep that are not of this coastal fold—in the middle of China." And to David Livingstone, "in the middle of Africa."

And just when all of western Christendom began to feel content in the twentieth century that every country of the world had been penetrated with the gospel, Jesus came to Cameron Townsend, the founder of Wycliffe Bible Translators, and said, in effect, "I have other sheep that are not of this visible worldwide fold—among the hidden tribal peoples, thousands of them with not even a portion of Scripture in their language."

John 10:16 is the great missionary text in the Gospel of John: Jesus has other sheep that are not of this fold! Every time we start to get comfortable with "just us," this is verse like a thorn in the pew cushion. Every time a board of world missions begins to get comfortable with the ten or eleven fields where they are planting churches, John 10:16 is like a bugle call: "I have other sheep," there among the thousands of peoples yet unreached by the gospel.

Four Reasons for Confidence

But this verse is far more than a mere goad. It is full of hope and power. It is a deep and broad foundation for great mission efforts. Let's look at four things in John 10:16 that should fill us to overflowing with confidence in our missions dreaming and planning and labor.

1. Christ has more sheep.

I have other sheep ...

There will always be people who argue that the doctrine of election and predestination makes missions pointless. But they are always wrong. It does not make missions pointless; it makes missions possible.

I remember John Alexander, a former president of InterVarsity, saying in a question-and-answer session at Urbana '67, "At the beginning of my missionary career, I said that if predestination were true I could not be a missionary. Now after twenty years of struggling with the hardness of the human heart, I say I could never be a missionary unless I believed in the doctrine of predestination."

"I have other sheep" gives hope that Christ most certainly has a people among the nations. They belong to his Father, and they will hear Jesus's voice. It was precisely this truth that encouraged the apostle Paul when he was downcast in Corinth. "And the Lord said to Paul one night in a vision, 'Do not be afraid, but go on speaking and do not be silent, for I am with you, and no one will attack you to harm you, for I have many in this city who are my people.'" (Acts 18:9–10)

"I have many in this city who are my people." "I have other sheep." These are promises full of hope for those who dream about new fields of missionary labor.

2. Christ's other sheep are scattered outside the present fold.

I have other sheep that are not of this fold.

John makes this point explicit in John 11:51–52, where he explains a word of prophecy spoken by Caiaphas, the high priest. Caiaphas had said, "It is better for you that one man should die for the people, not that the whole nation should perish" (John 11:50). Then John comments, "He did not say this of his own accord, but being high priest that year he prophesied that Jesus would die for the nation, and not for the nation only, but also to gather into one the children of God who are scattered abroad."

World evangelization, for the apostle John, is the ingathering of the children of God—those sheep whom God has chosen and intends to give to the Son. And the point for our encouragement in missionary strategy is that they are scattered. They are not all pocketed in one or two places; they are scattered everywhere. As John puts it in the book of Revelation, "You were slain, and by your blood you ransomed people for God from every tribe and language and people and nation" (Revelation 5:9).

This is why all the talk in our day about reaching unreached people groups is totally biblical. We may be sure, on the authority of God's word, that among all the peoples of the world we will find those who belong to the Father. What an encouragement to get on with the task of frontier missions and to reach all the unreached peoples of the world.

3. The Lord will bring his lost sheep home.

I must bring them also …

Jesus promises to gather all of his scattered sheep. He *will* bring them.

This does not mean, as some of the hyper-Calvinists thought it did in Carey's day, that Christ will gather in his sheep without sending us to call them. In John 20:21, Jesus says, "As the Father has sent me, even so I am sending you."

We continue the mission of Christ. Just as Jesus called his sheep with his own lips in Palestine, so he still calls them today with the lips of his people. Jesus's sheep hear his voice in our voices, and they follow him. Jesus does it. But not without us!

All authority in heaven and on earth has been given to the Son of God (Matthew 28:18), and he declares, "I must bring in my other sheep." He will do it. And that implies a final word of hope from the passage.

4. If he brings them, they will come.

I must bring them also, and they will listen to my voice.

None of Christ's sheep finally rejects his word. What else can keep a person going in a hard and unresponsive place of ministry except the confidence that God reigns and that those whom the Father has chosen will hear the voice of the Son?

Peter Cameron Scott was born in 1867 and founded the African Inland Mission. He had tried to serve in Africa, but he had to come home because he contracted malaria. The second attempt was especially joyful because he was joined by his brother John. But the joy evaporated as John fell victim to the fever. Scott buried his brother all by himself, and at the grave he rededicated himself to preach the gospel. But his health broke again, and he returned to England utterly discouraged.

But in London, something wonderful happened. Ruth Tucker tells the story in *From Jerusalem to Irian Jaya*.

> Back in England some months later, broken in health, he found inspiration again at the tomb of David Livingstone in Westminster Abbey as he knelt and read the inscription, "Other sheep I have which are not of this fold; them also I must bring." He would return to Africa and lay down his life, if need be, for the cause of which this great man had lived and died.[6]

---

6. Ruth Tucker, *From Jerusalem to Irian Jaya* (Grand Rapids, MI: Zondervan, 2004), 347.

Open Your Mouth

May God deepen and broaden the biblical foundation of our vision for the world. May he open our eyes, not only to the fields that are white to harvest, but also to the majesty and splendor and glory of his sovereign grace.

And may we be carried over all the obstacles and discouragements by the great confidence that the Lord himself will gather the ransomed from every tribe and tongue and people and nation. "I have other sheep that are not of this fold. I must bring them also. They will hear my voice!"

Don't waste your life. Open your mouth, and become a voice of the sovereign Shepherd.

ISAIAH 48:9-11

"For my name's sake I defer my anger; for the sake of my praise I restrain it for you, that I may not cut you off. [10]Behold, I have refined you, but not as silver; I have tried you in the furnace of affliction. [11]For my own sake, for my own sake, I do it, for how should my name be profaned? My glory I will not give to another."

4

A Rescue Mission from Glory to Gladness

The chief end of missions is the supremacy of God in the joy of all peoples.

You may recognize in that statement a paraphrase of the first question in the Westminster Catechism.

Question: What is the chief end of man?

Answer: Man's chief end is to glorify God, and to enjoy him forever.

So I have replaced "chief end of man" with "chief end of missions"—which seems legitimate because *missions* is shorthand for "man active in doing missions." There is no missions in the abstract without human action. There are only people doing missions. What is their chief end or goal? Or, what is God's chief end in their action?

Then I changed "to glorify God" to "the supremacy of God." The chief end of missions is the exaltation of God as *supremely* glorious—*supremely* beautiful and valuable above all other reality. The chief end of missions is the radical transformation of human hearts—through faith in Christ and through the work of the Holy Spirit—so that they treasure and magnify the glory of God *supremely* above all things. In that sense, the end of missions is the *supremacy* of God.

Then I changed "and enjoy him forever" to "the joy of all peoples." Missions is not just about winning your *neighbor* to Christ. It is about the *peoples* of the world. "Let the *peoples* praise you, O God; let all the *peoples* praise you!" (Psalm 67:3).

So the chief end of missions is *the glorification of God's supremacy in the jubilation of human hearts among all the peoples of the world*. Or we could say that the chief end of missions is the supremacy of God in the satisfaction of the peoples in God. Or that the chief end of missions is the glory of God in the God-centered gladness of the peoples.

Two Became One

But the most important change I made in the catechism was changing *and* to *in*. The catechism says, "Man's chief end is to glorify God, *and* to enjoy him forever." What does *and* mean here? If *and* means that there is one end of man called "glorify God" and another end of man called "enjoy him forever," then why did the authors of the catechism use the singular *end* when they answered, "The chief *end* of man is …"? Why didn't they say, "The chiefs *ends* of man *are* to glorify God, and to enjoy him forever"?

The answer is that the authors did *not* consider God's getting glory in man and man's getting joy in God as separate and distinct *ends*. They knew that God's being glorified in us and our being satisfied in him were one thing.

They *are* one thing—God's looking stunning *through* me is one thing with my being stunned *by* him. He looks stunning *in* my being stunned. God's being glorified and my enjoying him is one thing, in the same way that God's looking ravishing is one thing with my being ravished. God's being glorified and my enjoying him are one thing, in the same way that God's looking like the supreme treasure over all is one thing with my treasuring him as the supreme treasure over all. The world sees the supreme value of God in our valuing him supremely.

Those great Reformed theologians of the seventeenth century knew that God's being glorified in us and our being satisfied in him were not two separate goals of creation. They were one goal, one end. And so they wrote, "The chief *end* [not ends] of man is to glorify God, and to enjoy him forever." And what I am doing is simply making it explicit and clear *how* they are one in my paraphrase: "The chief end of missions is the supremacy of God *in* the joy of all peoples"—namely, the joy of all peoples in God.

When the peoples of the earth come to rejoice supremely in the Lord, the Lord will be supremely glorified in the peoples of the earth. There is one end, one aim, one goal of missions: the full and everlasting gladness of the peoples in the glory of God. Or, the glorification of God in the full and everlasting gladness of the peoples in God.

Rescue for Glory and Gladness

What does this most important change, from *and* to *in*, imply for our motivation in missions? It clarifies the relationship between the two great biblical motivations for doing missions: the joy you have in *seeing God glorified*, and the joy you have in *seeing people saved*—passion for the supremacy of God and compassion for perishing people.

Which do you have? Which is driving you? God's glory or man's good? God's worth or man's rescue? God's holiness or man's happiness? The exaltation of God's supremacy or the salvation of man's soul? What is your driving missions motivation?

Saying "the supremacy of God *in* the joy of all peoples" makes it clear that you don't have to choose between those two motives. In fact, you dare not choose. If you choose between them, both are canceled. They live and die together. Rightly understood, these two motives are one and not two.

When we say, "The chief end of missions is the supremacy of God *in* the joy of all peoples," we make plain that zeal for the supremacy of God *includes* zeal for the joy of all peoples. And the other way around: compassion for the joyless eternity of lost peoples *includes* a zeal for the glory of God. Rightly understood, it cannot be otherwise.

These are not separate motives, as if missions could be pursued with zeal for the glory God but no zeal for the joy of lost people! Or as if missions could be pursued with zeal for the joy of the lost but no zeal for the glory of God. No, that's not possible. Indifference to the glorification of God *is* indifference to the eternal joy of the peoples. Indifference to the eternal joy of the peoples *is* indifference to the glory of God. Because missions aims at the supremacy of God *in* the joy of all peoples—the joy of the peoples *in* God.

To be sure, not all people will be saved. Not all will enjoy God forever. Many will hate him to eternity. And

God will glorify his holy wrath in their righteous judgment. But that is *not* the goal of missions. Missions is a rescue movement to glorify God in the gladness of the peoples.

You Dare Not Choose

These are not two separate motives. They are one. "The chief end of missions is the supremacy of God *in* (not *and*) the joy of all peoples." You don't have to answer the question I asked a moment ago: "Which is driving you? God's glory or man's good? God's worth or man's rescue? God's holiness or man's happiness? The exaltation of God's supremacy or the salvation of man's soul?"

Stated like that, there is no right answer to that question. This *or* that. No, it's not this *or* that, but this *in* that. It's not God's glory *or* man's joy, but God's glory revealed *in* man's joy—man's joy *in* God. It's not God's worth *or* man's rescue, but God's worth revealed *in* man's rescue—his rescue from the deadly condition of not treasuring God's worth. God's worth is magnified when a person flees from a lifetime of belittling God's worth.

So you dare not choose between being motivated by your compassion for lost people and your zeal for the glory of God. If you know what the glory of God is, and you know what it means to be rescued from sin, then you will know that you must have *both* motives because they are one. The glory of God in the gladness of the peoples is one with the gladness of the peoples in the glory of God.

God's Word about God's Glory

Let's go to the Bible now and see if these things are so. Perhaps here is where the Holy Spirit will put the match to the kindling I am trying to lay.

All for the Sake of God's Name

The uniform and pervasive message of the Bible is that all things have been done *by God* for the glory of God, and all things should, therefore, be done *by us* for the glory of God. This doesn't mean we do them to *increase* his glory, but to *display* his glory, to *communicate* his glory—the supreme beauty of his manifold perfections.

When the apostle Paul comes to the end of the great explanation of redemptive history in Romans 9–11, he writes in Romans 11:36, "From him and through him and *to him* are all things. *To him* be glory forever." All things exist *to him*—that is, to his honor, to his fame, for the sake of his name and his praise. All things—absolutely all things, from microwave ovens to global missions, from the tiniest microbe to human cultures—all things are *to him*. To him be glory forever. All the peoples, all the languages, all the tribes are *to him*. They exist for him—his name, his praise, his honor, his glory.

Paul says again in Colossians 1:16, "All things were created through him and *for him*," referring to Christ. Everything in creation exists *for him*—for the honor of Christ, for the glory of Christ, for the name and the fame of Christ (see also Hebrews 2:10).

Or again, in Romans 1:5 Paul says, "We have received grace and apostleship to bring about the obedience of faith *for the sake of [Christ's] name* among all the nations." Paul's apostleship, and by extension the cause of missions, exists "for the sake of Christ's name among all the nations." For the name and honor and glory and fame of Jesus Christ.

This is where John Stott says in his commentary on Romans that the mission of the church exists, "for His Imperial Majesty, Jesus Christ, and for the glory of his empire."[7] For all we know, America may be a footnote in the history of the world someday, and every president virtually forgotten, just like the Caesars of Rome. (How many Caesars can you name? There were eighty.) But we know beyond all doubt that the name and the majesty and the kingdom of Christ, in the words of Daniel the prophet, "shall never be destroyed .... It shall break in pieces all these kingdoms and bring them to an end, and it shall stand forever" (Daniel 2:44).

God's Banner over Creation and Redemption

The point of all these texts—and dozens more like them— is that God's aim in creation is to put himself on display and to magnify the greatness of his glory. "The heavens declare the glory of God" (Psalm 19:1). He designed it that way. That is what the galaxies are for. And that is what everything that happens in creation is for. All of history, from creation to consummation, exists for the communication of the glory of God.

Isaiah 48:9–11 flies like a banner not just over God's rescue of Israel from exile, but over all his acts of rescue, especially the cross of Christ: "For my name's sake I defer

---

7. John R.W. Stott, *The Message of Romans: God's Good News for the World* (Downers Grove, IL: IVP, 1994), 53.

my anger; for the sake of my praise I restrain it for you, that I may not cut you off. Behold ... I have tried you in the furnace of affliction. For my own sake, for my own sake, I do it, for how should my name be profaned? My glory I will not give to another."

All of creation, all of redemption, all of history is designed by God to display God—to magnify the greatness of the glory of God. That is the ultimate goal of all things, including missions. The chief end of missions is the supremacy of God—the display and communication of the supreme worth and beauty of God.

God's Word about Our Gladness

But there is another stream of revelation flowing in the Bible concerning what God is up to in the world he has made and the world he is governing. He is seeking not only the glorification of his name; he is seeking the jubilation of the peoples *in* his name. Ponder this second stream of texts with me for a few moments.

Paul tells us in Romans 15:8 that the Son of God came to confirm God's promises to the Jews. But immediately he adds in verse 9, "and in order that the Gentiles [the non-Jewish peoples of the world] might glorify God for his mercy." And then he tells us what it means to glorify God for his mercy. He quotes four Old Testament passages about God's purpose for the joy of the nations.

> As it is written, "Therefore I will *praise* you
> among the Gentiles, and *sing* to your name."
> And again it is said, "*Rejoice*, O Gentiles, with
> his people." And again, "*Praise* the Lord, all you

Gentiles, and let all the peoples *extol* him." And
again Isaiah says, "The root of Jesse will come,
even he who arises to rule the Gentiles; in him
will the Gentiles *hope*." (Romans 15:9–12)

What does it mean that God's aim in missions is "that the
Gentiles might glorify God for his mercy"? Gather up all
his words! It means, let the peoples *praise*! Let the peoples
sing! Let the peoples *rejoice*! Let the peoples *extol*! Let
the peoples *hope*! It is unmistakable what God is up to in
history: the gladness of the peoples in God.

And if we go back to the Psalms, the purpose of God
for all the peoples of the earth is clear: joy in God above
all things.

Clap your hands, all peoples! Shout to God with
loud songs of joy! (Psalm 47:1)

Shout for joy to God, all the earth; sing the glory
of his name; give to him glorious praise. (Psalm
66:1–2)

Let the peoples praise you, O God; let all the
peoples praise you! Let the nations be glad and
sing for joy. (Psalm 67:3–4)

O kingdoms of the earth, sing to God; sing
praises to the Lord. (Psalm 68:32)

Oh sing to the LORD a new song; sing to the
LORD, all the earth! (Psalm 96:1)

The LORD reigns, let the earth rejoice; let the
many coastlands be glad! (Psalm 97:1)

Make a joyful noise to the LORD, all the earth;
break forth into joyous song and sing praises!
(Psalm 98:4)

Make a joyful noise to the LORD, all the earth!
(Psalm 100:1)

There is no doubt that God's global aim in creation and redemption is not only the glory of his name but also the gladness of the peoples. Specifically, the gladness of the peoples *in God*.

The Greatest of These Is Joy

And if someone asks, "Couldn't you do the same thing with faith and obedience and life? Couldn't you trace through all the Bible the places where God aims at these? Why not focus on those as the aim of God and the aim of missions?"

If you ask that, I would ask you, "Why do you think the great theologians who wrote the Westminster Catechism said, 'The chief end of man is to glorify God, and to *enjoy* him forever'?" Why didn't they say, "to glorify God and *trust* him forever"? Or "to glorify God and *obey* him forever"? Or "to glorify God and have *life* in him forever"?

Isn't the answer that the essence of faith and obedience and life—and indeed all genuine spiritual experience—is the enjoyment of God *in* those acts, such that if you remove the enjoyment of God from them, they cease to be God-exalting acts?

- Isn't the essence of *faith* the embrace of God in Christ as the all-sufficient satisfier of our souls—not just the giver of good gifts, but the giver himself? Isn't faith, at its essence, being satisfied with all that God is for us in Jesus (John 6:35)?

- And isn't *obedience*, with all its thousands of manifestations, at its essence, doing what God says with a view to enjoying more of God in the very doing of it and in the reward of it? For example, we obey the command to love our neighbor by expanding our joy in God in our neighbor's enjoyment of God. I would argue that such overflowing joy marks all God-exalting obedience (see also Hebrews 12:2; Acts 20:35; 2 Corinthians 9:7).

- And isn't the essence of eternal *life* to know God, as Jesus says in John 17:3? And what is knowing God in the fullest biblical sense? To know him like the devil knows him, with all the facts just right, but hating them? No. To know God in a saving way is to know his all-satisfying beauty and greatness and worth for what they really are: precious and soul-satisfying. To know him rightly is to treasure what is known.

If the enjoyment of God is withdrawn as an essential aspect of faith or obedience or life, they cease to be the goal of God. They cease to be what they are. Faith is not saving faith without being satisfied in all that God is for us in Christ. Obedience is not obedience where there's no obedience to the command, "Rejoice in the Lord always" (Philippians 4:4). And life is not life where God himself is not our delight.

Joined in Jesus Christ

So I say again, in creation and redemption and in the mission of the church, God aims supremely at both the glory of his name and the gladness of the peoples.

And in the fullness of time, the Son of God, Jesus Christ, came into the world to secure both of these goals. He came for the vindication of his Father's glory, and for the salvation of his Father's children. And he did this by dying on the cross and rising from the dead.

The night before he died, in great distress he said, "What shall I say? 'Father, save me from this hour'? But for this purpose I have come to this hour. Father, glorify your name." Then a voice came from heaven: "I have glorified it, and I will glorify it again" (John 12:27–28). Christ died for glory-belittling sinners to show that it would be true and clear that God does not sweep the dishonoring of his name under the rug of the universe. He died to vindicate the worth of his glory (Romans 3:23–26).

And he also came "to seek and to save the lost" (Luke 19:10). He said, "The Son of Man came ... to give his life as a ransom for many" (Mark 10:45). A ransom from everlasting misery to everlasting joy—"These things I have spoken to you, that my joy may be in you, and that your joy may be full" (John 15:11; see also 17:13). And at the end of the age, when all the peoples are gathered before Jesus, those who have received him as their treasure will hear the words, "Enter into the joy of your master" (Matthew 25:23). This is why he came: to purchase by his blood the joy of the peoples in the joy of their Master.

We Honor with Our Happiness

Jesus died for this: the glory of his Father and the gladness of his people. Frontier missions is an extension to the nations of Jesus's mission to the world. He came for the glory of the Father and the gladness of the peoples. So the chief end of missions is the supremacy of God and the joy of all peoples.

But not just *and*—rather, *in*. The aim of history, the aim of Christ in dying for sinners is the glory of God *in* the gladness of the nations. The chief end of missions is the supremacy of God *in* the joy of all peoples.

This is so because when you enjoy someone, you honor that person. You magnify their value. You glorify them. If I say to my wife, "It makes me happy to be with you," she doesn't accuse me of selfishness. Why not, since I just said that my motivation for being with her is my own happiness? Because when my happiness is in her, it calls attention to *her* worth, not mine. She is honored when I say, "It makes me happy to be with you." So is Christ. So is God the Father. They are seen to be a supreme treasure when they become for us our supreme pleasure. They are glorified in us when we are satisfied in them.

One Great Goal

Therefore, I say again that "the chief end of missions is the supremacy of God *in* the joy of all peoples." When the peoples find their supreme gladness in God, God will be supremely glorified in them. Which is why he created the world and why the cross of Jesus exists.

We will not choose between glorifying God and making people glad. We will not choose between praising God's supremacy and removing people's suffering—especially eternal suffering. We will not choose between hallowing God and helping people. In the aims of global missions, we will not choose between seeing Christ magnified among the peoples and seeing the peoples satisfied in Christ.

Because these two are one. Christ is supremely magnified in the peoples when the peoples are supremely satisfied in Christ. We have the best news in all the world: Jesus Christ, the Son of God, died and risen and reigning to make the nations fully and eternally glad in the glory of God.

When Christ becomes the satisfaction of the nations, and God becomes their delight, then he is honored and they are saved. And you—you who will take or send this best of all messages—you turn out to be a person of great compassion toward perishing sinners and a person of great zeal for the glory of God. Don't ever choose between these two: praising God and pitying sinners; divine glory and human gladness. Embrace this one great end, and give your life to it—the supremacy of God in the joy of all peoples.

EPHESIANS 3:1-13

For this reason I, Paul, a prisoner of Christ Jesus on behalf of you Gentiles— [2]assuming that you have heard of the stewardship of God's grace that was given to me for you, [3]how the mystery was made known to me by revelation, as I have written briefly. [4]When you read this, you can perceive my insight into the mystery of Christ, [5]which was not made known to the sons of men in other generations as it has now been revealed to his holy apostles and prophets by the Spirit. [6]This mystery is that the Gentiles are fellow heirs, members of the same body, and partakers of the promise in Christ Jesus through the gospel. [7]Of this gospel I was made a minister according to the gift of God's grace, which was given me by the working of his power. [8]To me, though I am the very least of all the saints, this grace was given, to preach to the Gentiles the unsearchable riches of Christ, [9]and to bring to light for everyone what is the plan of the mystery hidden for ages in God, who created all things, [10]so that through the church the manifold wisdom of God might now be made known to the rulers and authorities in the heavenly places. [11]This was according to the eternal purpose that he has realized in Christ Jesus our Lord, [12]in whom we have boldness and access with confidence through our faith in him. [13]So I ask you not to lose heart over what I am suffering for you, which is your glory.

5

The Unsearchable Riches of Christ for All Peoples

In this chapter we are going to move backward through Ephesians 3:8–10 in four steps. We will go from the widest view to the narrowest view, or from the biggest picture of things to the smallest, or from the greatest goal of missions backward through three successively smaller means to reach this great goal.

We will move from the display of God's great wisdom to the world of angels (v. 10), to the church gathered from all the nations (v. 10), to the preaching of the gospel of the riches of Christ (v. 9), to the simple sinner-saints who live and minister by grace alone—the missionaries (v. 8).

I go backward in this order because I want to end with us. God is not done with the work of missions. He said, "Go … and make disciples of all nations." And then he said, "I am with you always, to the end of the age" (Matthew 28:19–20). The promise is good until Jesus comes because the commission is binding until Jesus comes. Therefore, we all face a question: What is our role in obeying the Great Commission to reach all the unreached peoples of the world with the gospel of the riches of Christ?

Picture God's Mission

Picture in your mind a great, wise artist, painting on a huge canvas with many brushes, most of them very ordinary and messy. The painter is God, so you can't picture him. He's invisible. But he intends for his painting to be the visible display of his wisdom. He knows people can't see him, but he wants his wisdom to be seen and admired. His canvas is huge. It's the size of the created universe. I know you can't really imagine looking at that canvas because you are in it. But do your best.

God is painting with thousands and thousands of colors and shades and textures—a picture as big as the universe and as old as creation and as lasting as eternity—a picture we call history, with the central drama being the preparation, salvation, and formation of the church of Jesus Christ. And he is using thousands of different brushes, most of them very ordinary and very small because every minute detail is crucial in this painting; every stroke displays the wisdom of the Painter. These brushes are God's missionaries.

There's a reason from the text that I am encouraging you to have a picture like this in your mind. It's in the word *manifold* in verse 10: "so that through the church the manifold wisdom of God might now be made known to the rulers and authorities in the heavenly places."

This Greek word for *manifold* occurs in the Bible only here. It is very unusual. Half of it (*poikilos*) means "wrought

in various colors"—diversified, intricate, complex, subtle.
Then Paul puts a prefix on the word that means *many*
(*polupoikilos*). The word brings to mind very many colors
and variations and intricacies and subtleties. Since that
is in the text, I want you to think of the display of God's
wisdom as a universe-sized painting with innumerable
colors and shadings and texture. It is unsearchably intricate.

1. The Display of God's Manifold Wisdom

Let's start our four steps in verse 10, where Paul tells us the
greatest goal of history and missions. You can see from the
words *so that* that God's purpose and aim for missions and
the church are now being expressed. The riches of Christ
are preached to the Gentiles, the nations, and the church is
gathered from all the peoples "*so that* through the church
the manifold wisdom of God might now be made known
to the rulers and authorities in the heavenly places."

This is God's goal. This is why he created the world,
why he redeemed a people through the death of his Son
(Ephesians 2:12–19), and why he sends missionaries and
gathers his church by the preaching of the riches of Christ.
This is the central drama of history, and this is the goal of
missions.

This universe is finally about the many-colored
wisdom of God. History exists to display the infinitely
varied and complex and intricate wisdom of God. Missions is the means that God uses to gather the church.
And that gathering from all the nations is the focus of this
wisdom-displaying painting. You see that in the words
through the church: "so that through the church the manifold wisdom of God might now be made known."

If this gathering of the church is God's painting, then

who is the audience? Paul says that God is making his
wisdom known "to the rulers and authorities in the heavenly places." This means that the painting, and the drama
of history and redemption that it portrays, from creation
to consummation, is meant to show angels—the good ones
and the evil ones—the greatness of God's wisdom.

Missions, the ingathering of God's elect, and the
church exist so that the worship of heaven would be white
hot with admiration and wonder. Of course, no angel in
God's presence will ever sing, "Amazing grace, how sweet
the sound that saved a wretch like me." They are not
wretches and have never been lost. This is our song and our
joy, and they can never sing it or know it. But God wanted
them to see it. And the angels love to stoop down and get
as close as they can to the wonders of redemption and how
God prepared and saved and gathered his church (1 Peter
1:12).

And the demons (Ephesians 6:12), the evil rulers
and authorities, must look at this painting and watch the
wisdom by which they were defeated in the very moment
they thought they had triumphed—in the death and
resurrection of Christ, and in the blood of the martyrs. As
Jesus says in Revelation 2:10, "Behold, the devil is about
to throw some of you into prison, that you may be tested,
and for ten days you will have tribulation. Be faithful unto
death, and I will give you the crown of life."

Just when God paints with the dark color of death,
and the devils begin to gloat, God picks up another brush
and with orange and yellow and red makes that dark death
serve the beauty of his wisdom. And the demons gnash
their teeth.

So every brush stroke on God's painting will add to

the infinitely intricate display of his wisdom to the armies of heaven.

2. The Gathering of God's Global Church

We have seen in verse 10 that it is *through the church* that the divine Painter is displaying his manifold wisdom to the armies of heaven and hell. Notice now that the church is being gathered from *all the nations*. Paul writes, "To me, though I am the very least of all the saints, this grace was given, to preach to the Gentiles [that is, the non-Jewish nations] the unsearchable riches of Christ, and to bring to light for everyone what is the plan of the mystery hidden for ages in God, who created all things" (vv. 8–9)

The "mystery hidden for ages" is this universal scope of the gospel that includes Gentiles, not just Jews, in the covenant people of God. Paul makes this crystal clear in verse 6: "This mystery is that the Gentiles are fellow heirs, members of the same body, and partakers of the promise in Christ Jesus through the gospel." The nations share in the promise made to Abraham. They become part of the historic people of God. They become true Jews (Romans 2:29).

Paul makes this same point in Romans 11. Wild Gentile branches are being grafted into the tree of promise, and broken-off Jewish branches will be grafted in when the fullness of the Gentiles comes in (Romans 11:17–27). As Paul contemplates the strange and intricate way that God is saving his church from all the nations, he comes to the same place in Romans 11:33 as he does in Ephesians 3:10—namely, to the praise of God's unsearchable wisdom: "Oh, the depth of the riches and wisdom and knowledge of God! How unsearchable are his judgments and how inscrutable his ways!"

That is what God aims at in heaven and on earth—the praise of his many-colored wisdom in the way he is saving and gathering his church from all the peoples of the world. There are twists and turns in history that bring about God's design in ways that no one ever dreamed. There are no wasted strokes on this canvas as God paints his wisdom in the history of missions.

3. The Preaching of Christ's Unsearchable Riches

That leads us now to the means of this gathering. How does missions advance? How is the church gathered from the nations to the praise of God's many-colored wisdom?

In Ephesians 3:8–9, Paul writes, "To me, though I am the very least of all the saints, this grace was given, to preach to the Gentiles the unsearchable riches of Christ, and to bring to light for everyone what is the plan of the mystery hidden for ages in God, who created all things."

Missions happens by preaching to the nations "the unsearchable riches of Christ." Missionaries lift up Jesus Christ and all that God is for us in him, and God gathers his elect from all the peoples of the world.

That phrase, "the unsearchable riches of Christ," is worth a whole book. But I will give one pointer to what it means. In Ephesians 2:12, Paul tells the Gentiles, "Remember that you were at that time separated from Christ, alienated from the commonwealth of Israel and strangers to the covenants of promise, having no hope and without God in the world."

Once, all that God had ever promised in the Old Testament for the glorious future of his people was not theirs.

The Gentiles were excluded from all of it. But because of the gospel message, based on the cross of Christ, Paul writes, "you are no longer strangers and aliens, but you are fellow citizens with the saints and members of the household of God" (Ephesians 2:19).

That is what missionaries preach everywhere they go: "You Uzbeks, you Maninka, you Kachin, you Shandai, you Swedes, you Germans, you Russians, you British—you who trust Christ are now part of the covenant made with Israel. You are fellow citizens. You are members of the household of God. You will inherit every promise ever made if you believe in Christ. All of them are Yes to you in Christ (2 Corinthians 1:20). You will inherit the earth. You are heirs of the world. You are children of the Maker of the universe in Jesus Christ. All things are yours. And Jesus Christ is the sum of all those things, and all things will show you more of him and increase your joy forever."

Ephesians 2:7 says that it is going to take eternity for God to exhaust on you the unsearchable riches of his glory in Christ Jesus. It will take ages upon ages upon ages for the riches of Christ to be searched out.

That is what missionaries say and show to the nations of the world: that Christ died and rose again so that people from every nation might be one in this inheritance.

Which leaves just one final question—who are the brushes? If God aims to display his many-colored wisdom with the canvas of world history, and if the ingathering of the church from every people and tribe and nation is the main drama on this canvas, and if missions is the means of gathering and establishing that church among all the peoples, who are the brushes God uses to paint this drama?

4. The Service of God's Ordinary Missionaries

The brushes he uses are messy, ordinary people who have seen the unsearchable riches of Christ and are willing, and often eager, to take these riches to the nations. The brushes are broken, sinning, ordinary missionaries—of whom the world is not worthy (Hebrews 11:38).

In Ephesians 3:8, Paul says, "To me, though I am the very least of all the saints, this grace was given, to preach to the Gentiles the unsearchable riches of Christ."

Paul mentions that he is the least of all the saints for two reasons. One reason is because he was a hater and persecutor of the church and of Christ. He never got over that God had chosen him despite his horrible past. The other reason is to remind you today that he can do the same for you.

So here is one of the greatest incentives of all to give ourselves to missions. God intends to use ordinary, messy, small paint brushes on the canvas of the history of missions because every minute stroke of his brush matters. Every bright stroke of triumph and every dark stroke of suffering matters. He is an infinitely wise painter. He knows what he is doing with your life. Not one stroke will be wasted. You can trust him with your life. Yield to the wise hand that would paint with your life.

PSALM 67

May God be gracious to us
and bless us and make his face to shine upon us,
^{2}that your way may be known on earth,
your saving power among all nations.
^{3}Let the peoples praise you, O God;
let all the peoples praise you!
^{4}Let the nations be glad and sing for joy,
for you judge the peoples with equity
and guide the nations upon earth.
^{5}Let the peoples praise you, O God;
let all the peoples praise you!
^{6}The earth has yielded its increase;
God, our God, shall bless us.
^{7}God shall bless us;
let all the ends of the earth fear him!

Let the Peoples Praise You, O God! Let All the Peoples Praise You!

Before we begin, let me make two brief comments. First, Psalm 67 is the way we pray when we are besotted with God's zeal for his praise among all the peoples of the world. One of the barometers of the fruitfulness of this book is whether you are more inclined to pray like this now than you were before you began reading.

Second, God often alters the course of our lives by causing a portion of his word to take root in us, grow, and not wither. It hangs on. It revives again and again. It survives from season to season. It does something to us. We can't shake it. It holds us. It changes things. We can't fully explain it, but it becomes a call of God on our lives. May the Lord make Psalm 67 such a text for you.

The way verses 1 and 2 relate to each other roots this psalm firmly in the way God is at work in history to save the world. Notice the connection between God's blessing Israel (that's the *us* of verse 1) and Israel's being a blessing to the nations (v. 2): "May God be gracious to us and *bless us* [note those words!] and make his face to shine upon us, *that* [this is the aim of God in blessing Israel] your way may be known on earth, your saving power among *all nations.*"

Rooted in God's Covenant

This connection between being blessed and being a blessing to the nations means that the psalmist is rooting his prayer in Genesis 12:2–3. God promises to Abraham, "I will make of you a great nation, and I will *bless* you and make your name great, so that you will *be a blessing.* I will *bless* those who bless you, and him who dishonors you I will curse, and *in you all the families of the earth shall be blessed.*"

So this prayer in Psalm 67 is not hanging in the air with no connections to God's historical way of saving the world. It is rooted in God's covenant with Abraham. It brings that covenant up to date and prays it into reality. That is what we are supposed to do with God's covenants— his promises. We are to bring them up to date and pray them into reality.

So let's do that—into the twenty-first century. I think the psalmist, and Abraham, would be upset with us if we didn't. The decisive fulfillment of God's covenant with Abraham—not the final fulfillment, but the decisive one— was the life and death and resurrection of Jesus Christ, the offspring of Abraham (Galatians 3:16). And because Jesus in all his saving work is the seed of Abraham, everyone— including people from the most pagan nations—who is united to him by faith becomes a son of Abraham and an heir of all his blessings.

> Christ redeemed us from the curse of the law
> by becoming a curse for us ... so that in Christ
> Jesus the blessing of Abraham might come to
> the Gentiles [the nations!]. (Galatians 3:13–14)

> Know then that it is those of faith who are the
> sons of Abraham ... So then, those who are of
> faith are blessed along with Abraham, the man
> of faith .... If you are Christ's, then you are
> Abraham's offspring, heirs according to promise.
> (Galatians 3:7, 9, 29)

Psalm 67 in the Twenty-First Century

So God's plan was that all the peoples of the world be blessed. To that end, he chose the people of Israel to bear his revelation and his blessing. And he made a covenant with them so that they would be blessed and then bring that blessing to all the peoples of the world. And God fulfilled this covenant decisively when Jesus Christ, the seed of Abraham, fulfilled all righteousness and died for sin and rose again, so that anyone who believes on him from any people on earth will become a child of Abraham and inherit the blessing of Abraham—and so be blessed by the blessing of Israel. So the Abrahamic covenant is being fulfilled every time someone trusts Christ.

So we are going to read this prayer in Psalm 67 as part of the ongoing historical realization of this great covenant, and its decisive fulfillment in Jesus, and its ongoing fulfillment through the church. The prayer is really meant to be read as a realization of the covenant with Abraham and as an expression of how that covenant would be fulfilled in us today through Jesus Christ.

God's Great Purpose for the World

The first thing we'll look at in the prayer is God's great purpose for the world and all its thousands of people groups. God inspired this prayer (which Jesus says about the Psalms in Matthew 22:43), so we can see in it not just the *psalmist's* purpose, but *God's* great purpose for the world he made.

According to Psalm 67, God's purpose is to be *known* and *praised* and *enjoyed* and *feared* among all the peoples of the earth. This is why he created the world, why he chose Israel, why Christ died, and why missions exists. Missions exists because the knowledge of God, the praise of God, the enjoyment of God, and the fear of God don't exist among the nations.

Let me point out each of these.

1. God's purpose is to be *known* among all the nations. "That your way may be known on earth, your saving power among all nations" (v. 2).
2. His purpose is to be *praised* among all the nations. "Let the peoples praise you, O God; let all the peoples praise you!" (v. 3). "Let the peoples praise you, O God; let all the peoples praise you!" (v. 5).
3. God's purpose is to be *enjoyed* among all the peoples. "Let the nations be glad and sing for joy" (v. 4).
4. His purpose is to be *feared*, or reverenced, among all the nations. "Let all the ends of the earth fear him!" (v. 7).

This psalmist is praying in accord with the will of God. That's what it means to speak "in the Spirit," as Jesus says the psalmists do. Therefore, we don't just see the purpose of a man in this prayer, but the purpose of God. God's aim in his creation is that he would be *known* and *praised* and *enjoyed* and *reverenced* among all the peoples of the earth. That's why the world exists. And that's why missions exists.

Why This Great Purpose?

But the psalm tells us more about God's purpose for the world. It shows us four things he aims to be *known* for and *praised* for, what it is about him he means for all nations to *enjoy*, and why we should reverence him and *fear* turning away from him to another god.

1. He Is God Alone

First, God aims to be known as the one and only true and living God.

He is not the God of any other religion. I gather this from the fact that an inspired Israelite poet is praying that *his* God will be known and praised among all the peoples who worship other gods. "Let the peoples praise *you*, O God; let all the peoples praise *you*!" (v. 3). The God of Israel said in Isaiah 45:5–6, "I am the LORD, and there is no other, besides me there is no God; I equip you, though you do not know me, that people may know, from the rising of the sun and from the west, that there is none besides me; I am the LORD, and there is no other."

If this is not true, missions would be the most audacious and presumptuous enterprise in the world. Calling the nations to know and praise and enjoy and fear one God alone, the God of Israel, the God and Father of our Lord Jesus Christ, would be arrogant and presumptuous, if it's not true that he's the one and only true God. But if it is true, then missions is a humble, daring, obedient response of a people who love those who are perishing.

The psalmist does not pray, "May all the nations become sincere worshipers of their gods since all gods are one." Let's be crystal clear here: in a world supercharged with the presence of Islam, it does not help the cause of truth or love to say that we worship the same God—and I am putting the emphasis there on *worship*. We do not worship the same God.

Muslims do not believe in a Jesus who died, who gave his life as a ransom, who rose from the dead, and who claimed to be the divine Son of God. All those things are rejected by Islam. The historical Jesus of the Gospels is denied by Muslims in at least those four critical ways.

And Jesus speaks clearly about people (of whatever religion—Christian or Muslim) who deny him in this way. He says:

a. *They do not know the true God*: "You know neither me nor my Father. If you knew me, you would know my Father also" (John 8:19; see also 7:28; 14:7).
b. *They do not honor the true God*: "Whoever does not honor the Son does not honor the Father who sent him" (John 5:23).
c. *They do not love the true God*: "I know that you do not have the love of God within you. I have come in my Father's name, and you do not receive me" (John 5:42–43).

> d. *They do not have the true God*: "No one who denies the Son has the Father. Whoever confesses the Son has the Father also" (1 John 2:23).
>
> e. *They have not heard or learned from the true God*: "Everyone who has heard and learned from the Father comes to me" (John 6:45).
>
> f. *They reject the true God*: "The one who rejects me rejects him who sent me" (Luke 10:16).

Neither Muslims nor anyone else (including those who call themselves Christians) truly worships God if they reject Jesus as he really is in the Gospels.

Psalm 67 is a prayer that all the religions of the world, including Islam (which came into being perhaps sixteen hundred years after this psalm) would turn and know and praise and enjoy and fear the one and only true God—the God and Father of the Messiah, Jesus. And Jesus endorsed this prayer with his own blood.

Jesus came into the world to awaken and save those who rejected him—like we all once did. "I came not to call the righteous, but sinners" (Mark 2:17). And Jesus says, "So I am sending you" (John 20:21)! He is sending out ambassadors today to all the Muslim peoples (and all the other religions), saying, "I love you. Come to me and believe in me and I will give you life. My purpose is to be known and praised and enjoyed and feared as the one true God—Jesus Christ."

So the first thing God wants the nations to know about him is that he is the one and only true God.

2. He Is a God of Justice

Second, he wants the nations to know that he is a God of justice. "Let the nations be glad and sing for joy, for you *judge the peoples with equity*" (v. 4).

When the judgment of the nations comes, God will not be partial. No one will be condemned for the color of his skin, or the size of his brain, or the place of his birth, or the quality of his ancestry.

No bribes or sophisticated plea bargaining will be considered. All will proceed on the basis of God's unimpeachable righteousness. Let this be known to all the peoples of the earth. They will stand on an equal footing with Israel when it comes to judgment. The standard of justice will be the same for both.

The standard of acceptance—God's standard of vindication in the court of heaven—will be perfection. And the only remedy for our universal failure and rebellion is the *perfection of Jesus, which he performed* for all who believe in him, and the *punishment of Jesus, which he endured* for all who believe in him. Jesus's perfect obedience to God is not one remedy among others—the remedy just for people in the Christian tribe. It is the only remedy for all the descendants of Adam. "As by the one man's disobedience the many were made sinners, so by the one man's obedience the many will be made righteous" (Romans 5:19). If a person has embraced Christ as his only hope before God, he will be saved. If he has not, he will be lost.

And God will not be unjust toward those who have never heard the preaching of the gospel. They will not be judged for not believing in a Jesus they never heard of. They will be judged for how they have responded to the revelation they have. And Romans 1 tells us there will be no excuse. None is righteous. None submits to God's truth outside Christ.

> The wrath of God is revealed from heaven against all ungodliness and unrighteousness of men, who by their unrighteousness suppress the truth. For what can be known about God is plain to them, because God has shown it to them. For his invisible attributes, namely, his eternal power and divine nature, have been clearly perceived, ever since the creation of the world, in the things that have been made. So they are without excuse. For although they knew God, they did not honor him as God or give thanks to him. (Romans 1:18–21)

God aims to be known as a God of justice. The God of all the earth will do right. He will judge the peoples with equity—either in hell or in Jesus.

3. He Is a God of Power

Third, God aims to be known for his sovereign power.

We see this in the last part of verse 4: "Let the nations be glad and sing for joy, for you judge the peoples with equity *and guide the nations upon earth.*" Many nations boast of their power and their independence as sovereign states. And when they do, the Lord laughs because he made the nations; he determined their allotted periods of time and the boundaries of their dwelling place (Acts 17:26).

> The king's heart is a stream of water in the hand of the LORD; he turns it wherever he will. (Proverbs 21:1)

He removes kings and sets up kings. (Daniel 2:21)

He does according to his will among the host
of heaven and among the inhabitants of the
earth; and none can stay his hand, or say to him,
"What have you done?" (Daniel 4:35)

God aims to make himself known as supremely sovereign
among all the nations—specifically that he runs the world.
He is the guide of the nations. They are not sovereign.
Only One is sovereign. And he sets the destiny of every
nation.

And part of that destiny is that they hear the gospel.
To that end, Jesus said, "All authority in heaven and on
earth has been given to me. Go therefore and make disciples of all nations ... And behold, I [the sovereign one
with all authority] am with you always, to the end of the
age" (Matthew 28:18–20).

"My will is that the nations be discipled," Jesus essentially says. "All of them. And not only is this duty my will
of command, but this destiny is my will of decree. I will
build my church!"

4. He Is a God of Grace

Fourth and finally, God aims to be known as a gracious
God.

The only true God, who is just in all his judgment and
sovereign in all his rule, is a God of grace. He wants to be
known this way. We see this in verse 1: "May God be gracious to us and bless us and make his face to shine upon us,
that your way may be known on earth, your saving power
[literally, *salvation*] among all nations."

He aims to be known as a God who is *gracious* and

who *saves*. And this doesn't mean "who is gracious only to Israel," because verse 4 says, "Let the *nations* be glad." If the grace of God were only for Israel, there would be no gladness for the nations.

This is why the news that resounds through the world from the cross of Jesus onward is called *gospel*. It is good news. It is news of the God of grace. Paul said that with the coming of Christ into the world "the grace of God has appeared, bringing salvation for all people" (Titus 2:11). And when he summed up his life and ministry, he said it was all about the gospel of grace: "I do not account my life of any value nor as precious to myself, if only I may finish my course and the ministry that I received from the Lord Jesus, to testify to the *gospel of the grace of God*" (Acts 20:24).

The heart of the missionary message to the nations is this: God will save you from your sin and guilt and condemnation by grace through faith in his Son Jesus Christ. We go with a message of grace, not a message of condemnation.

The Mission Will Be Finished

To sum up what we've seen: God's great purpose in the world is to be known and praised and enjoyed and feared. And the truth about him, what he wants to be known and praised and enjoyed and feared for, is that

- he is the one and only true and living God, the Father of Jesus Christ;
- he is infinitely just and holy in all his ways, settling all accounts justly either on the cross for believers or in hell for those who reject his truth;

- he is sovereign over all the affairs of men and nations, and over the saving mission of his church through the all-authoritative, risen Christ; and
- he is a God of boundless grace to all who come to him through Jesus.

Because he is gracious, he *aims* to be known among all the peoples. And because he is sovereign, he *will* be known among all the peoples.

> "I will build my church, and the gates of hell shall not prevail against it." (Matthew 16:18)

> "I have other sheep that are not of this fold. I *must* bring them also, and they *will* listen to my voice. So there will be one flock, one shepherd." (John 10:16)

> "This gospel of the kingdom *will* be proclaimed throughout the whole world as a testimony to all nations." (Matthew 24:14)

This is the great hope and confidence that created the missionary movement of the Christian church. And this is the hope and confidence that will sustain us until we finish the mission. And it *will* be finished.

Earth's Harvest

There is one final point that needs to be made from Psalm 67—from the beginning and ending of this psalm. The psalm begins and ends with the connection between the people of God being blessed by God and the nations being blessed by us. We saw this in verses 1–2: "May God be gracious to us and bless us and make his face to shine upon us, *that* your way may be known on earth, your saving power among all nations."

What we have not yet noticed is that when the connection is repeated at the end of the psalm, it is harvest time, and the blessing on the people of God is mainly a material blessing. "The earth has yielded its increase; God, our God, shall bless us. God shall bless us; let all the ends of the earth fear him!" (vv. 6–7).

So the immediate blessing in view is the way God has provided all the material needs of his people. "The earth has yielded its increase" (v. 6).

God Is What Matters

And the amazing thing is that between the beginning blessing and the closing blessing in this psalm, the entire focus is not on material blessings for the world but spiritual ones—that is, God himself. Derek Kidner in his commentary says,

> If the setting of the psalm ... seems to be a festival of harvest home, it is remarkable ... how nature is overshadowed by history, and the psalmist [is] stirred by hopes that have no material or self-regarding element .... Here, nothing matters but man's need of God himself.[8]

The pervasive concern for the nations is that they would know and praise and enjoy and fear the true God—God himself.

---

8. Derek Kidner, *Psalms 1–72*, vol. 15 of the *Tyndale Old Testament Commentary* (Downers Grove, IL: IVP Academic, 2008), 236.

Which means this, at least: God gives his people *material wealth* for the sake of the world's *spiritual worship.* That is, he blesses his church with riches for the sake of reaching the nations. He gives a bountiful wheat harvest for the sake of a bountiful world harvest. He gives us more money than we need so that we can meet the world's greatest need—the need to know God through Jesus Christ.

This is the sharpest point of this psalm. We are blessed to be a blessing. And, of course, that means we are spiritually blessed. But in this psalm, the Lord has something more specifically to say—especially to the American church and the church of the West.

Blessings Doubled in Going and Giving

What does God have to say to us? We could put it like this.

I have blessed you, beyond the wildest dreams of any people in history. I have blessed you with unprecedented and overflowing wealth. This not a curse. It is a blessing. But it will become a curse if you do not use it for what I have designed.

And what I have designed is not that you lose and they gain. What I have designed is that you go and you give, and both gain. I love you, and I love the nations. I have blessed you, and I mean to double your blessing by making you a blessing. It is more blessed to give than to receive (Acts 20:35). That's the way I created you. Therefore my design—"blessed to be a blessing"—is for your joy and their joy. When I bless you that you may be a blessing, I bless you that your joy may be full.

When I say, "Let the nations be glad!" I mean, "Let your

gladness be doubled in their gladness." This is why I have blessed you. Don't turn my blessing into a curse. Don't put it in a bag with holes. I have blessed you. This is why you are rich—"that my way may be known on earth, my saving power among all nations."

"Let the peoples praise you, O God; let all the peoples praise you! Let the nations be glad and sing for joy" (vv. 5–6). For this we have been blessed. This is our mission. This is our joy. No matter what it costs.

2 CORINTHIANS 2:12-17

When I came to Troas to preach the gospel of Christ, even though a door was opened for me in the Lord, [13]my spirit was not at rest because I did not find my brother Titus there. So I took leave of them and went on to Macedonia. [14]But thanks be to God, who in Christ always leads us in triumphal procession, and through us spreads the fragrance of the knowledge of him everywhere. [15]For we are the aroma of Christ to God among those who are being saved and among those who are perishing, [16]to one a fragrance from death to death, to the other a fragrance from life to life. Who is sufficient for these things? [17]For we are not, like so many, peddlers of God's word, but as men of sincerity, as commissioned by God, in the sight of God we speak in Christ.

7

The Aroma of Christ among the Nations

Before we turn to the text from 2 Corinthians, let me put the passage in a missionary context. The apostle Paul was a missionary. We see that with crystal clarity in Romans 15:20, where he says that his ambition—his holy ambition—was "to preach the gospel, not where Christ has already been named, lest I build on someone else's foundation."

He was called to the frontiers, where the church was not yet established. We call this *frontier* missions, or *pioneer* missions, or missions to *unreached people groups*. Paul was the first and probably the greatest. But oh, what a lineage of lovers followed in his train, right down to this day.

Missions for Two Thousand Years

You can state the reason for this two-thousand-year lineage of missionaries in many different ways.

For example, before Jesus went back to heaven, he told his disciples, "All authority in heaven and on earth has been given to me. Go therefore and make disciples of all nations … And behold, I am with you always, to the end of the age" (Matthew 28:18–20). He has all authority over the souls of all people and nations, he promises to be with us to help us, and he commands us to go. That is valid today because the end of the age has not come.

Or you can give the reason for missions like the psalmist does: "Sing to the LORD, bless his name; tell of his salvation from day to day. Declare his glory among the nations, his marvelous works among all the peoples!" (Psalm 96:2–3). God created the world to display and magnify his glory. People who don't believe don't magnify the glory of his grace. We want them to. We want "the earth [to] be filled with the knowledge of the glory of the Lord as the waters cover the sea (Habakkuk 2:14).

Or you can give the reason for missions like this: "For God so loved the world, that he gave his only Son, that whoever believes in him should not perish but have eternal life" (John 3:16). The love of God extends salvation to all. Everyone who believes in Jesus has eternal life with Jesus, and everyone who doesn't perishes. Missions is the answer of our heart to that love.

Or you can give the reason for missions like this: According to the rigorous statistical efforts of the Joshua Project, there are nearly sixteen thousand distinct ethnolinguistic peoples in the world. Of these, they count nearly eight thousand as unreached; that is, fewer than two percent of them are Christians. About three billion people live in those unreached people groups.

Of the one hundred largest unreached people groups,

forty-four are in India, eight are in China, and seven are in Indonesia and Pakistan. The three largest are the Japanese in Japan, the Bengali in Bangladesh, and the Shaikh in India. Of these one hundred largest unreached peoples, forty-three are Muslim, thirty-six are Hindu, and nine are Buddhist. Twenty-two of them have populations over twenty million. In other words, there is a great work to be done in obedience to Jesus. And Jesus has all authority to get it done.

When I was a pastor, one of my great longings was that my church would be the sending base of ever-increasing numbers of missionaries to the unreached peoples, and that we would send them with ever-increasing effectiveness and ever-increasing biblical faithfulness and ever-increasing care for them and their families. When I thought about not wasting my life, this is what I would think about as often as anything: study and pray and write and speak and lead in a way that results in more and more visionary young people and restless mid-career people and wise, mature, retired people pulling up their stakes, packing their tents, and going with Jesus and the gospel to unreached peoples of the world, no matter where they are, far or near.

So with passion in mind, and praying as we go, let's look at one missionary's testimony. Keep in mind that God often—very often—uses his word to awaken and confirm his calling to the work of missions. May that happen now, as I simply unfold 2 Corinthians 2:12–17.

Leaving an Open Door

The situation behind this text is that Paul wrote a painful letter to Corinth and is anxious about whether it had

alienated them or healed them. So he sent Titus to
Corinth to find out how they were doing. It may help to
have the geography clear: Corinth is in the southern tip
of Greece. If you go up the east coast, you come to the
northern part of the peninsula called Macedonia, where
Thessalonica and Philippi are. Just to the east, across the
Aegean Sea, which separates Greece and Turkey today, was
Troas.

This is where we pick up the story. "When I came to
Troas to preach the gospel of Christ, even though a door
was opened for me in the Lord, my spirit was not at rest
because I did not find my brother Titus there. So I took
leave of them and went on to Macedonia" (vv. 12–13).

So even though there was an open door for the gospel
in Troas, Paul's heart was so troubled by the situation in
Corinth that he decided not to stay but to keep moving to
where he might meet Titus on the way back from Corinth.

I'm not going to linger here, but this is very striking
and may relate to where you are in your life. A door is
wide open where you are. Much needs to be done—right
where you are. But your spirit cannot rest. So it was with
Paul. And amazingly, he left the open door of Troas
behind and followed his restless spirit. Should he have left
Troas? Should you? He did. And because he did, we have
this amazing portion of Scripture.

Conquered in Christ

Paul eventually reaches Macedonia, and at last Titus comes.
He doesn't say that in this passage, but he does later in his
epistle.

> For even when we came into Macedonia, our
> bodies had no rest, but we were afflicted at every
> turn—fighting without and fear within. But
> God, who comforts the downcast, comforted
> us by the coming of Titus, and not only by his
> coming but also by the comfort with which
> he was comforted by you, as he told us of your
> longing, your mourning, your zeal for me, so that
> I rejoiced still more. (2 Corinthians 7:5–7)

That's the context of chapter 2. But here in chapter 2, Paul exults in a very different way. He chooses two shocking metaphors. First, he says in verse 14, "But thanks be to God, who in Christ always leads us in triumphal procession." This doesn't mean what you probably think it means. The word translated "leads in triumphal procession" (*thriambeuonti*) refers to what a great Roman general does when he leads in captivity those enemies he has conquered, taking them to their death or to slavery.

The word is used one other place in the New Testament, in Colossians 2:15: "[God] disarmed the rulers and authorities and put them to open shame, by triumphing over [*thriambeusas*] them in him." So in Colossians, Paul says God leads the devil in triumph, and in 2 Corinthians, he says that God leads Paul in triumph. Both have been defeated in their rebellion against God. Both are being led in triumphal procession and shamed for their rebellion.

But the great difference is that Paul is in Christ and Satan is not. Paul was defeated and taken captive, but he was brought to faith, forgiven, justified, and made a glad and willing servant of the greatest General who ever was. Paul was in Christ, and that makes all the difference.

A Picture with Two Purposes

So why does he use this word picture? Because he wants to accomplish two almost opposite things at the same time. One the one hand, God is triumphant, and Paul is in his service. But on the other hand, God is like a great General, and Paul is conquered and called to suffer in his service—even die. That's what this word picture accomplishes.

One the one hand, Paul wants to rejoice and thank God that the Corinthians have repented and that his painful letter did not alienate them but blessed them. That's a triumph worth exulting over with a triumphal procession.

But on the other hand, he knows that there are many adversaries in Corinth who do not accept his authority as an apostle and who have preached a different gospel (2 Corinthians 11:4). He calls them "super-apostles" in 11:5 and 12:11. They don't recognize Paul's authority, and they don't see Christ in his ministry.

In other words, Paul knows that he is not triumphant as a missionary the way some think he should be. Some people are converted, and some are not. Some see Christ in him, and some see only weakness. He has some success and some failure. So he chooses a word picture that describes him both as belonging to a great Victor, and as a conquered enemy whose service of the king is to suffer and look weak and even die for him—to be led in triumphal procession as a defeated foe in the service of the King.

A Sacrifice Pleasing to God

That's the first picture. The second picture is of his life as a sacrificial offering that has a sweet fragrance before God.

This picture starts in the middle of verse 14: "Through us [he] spreads the fragrance of the knowledge of him everywhere."

Paul pictures his missionary life and ministry as spreading a fragrance of the knowledge of Christ. And I say it is a picture of a sacrifice being offered to God because Paul says that the aroma is first "to God." Paul's ministry is like incense being offered to God: "For we are the aroma of Christ to God" (v. 15). Not first to the world, but to God.

Ephesians 5:2 gives the best explanation of this picture: "Christ loved us and gave himself up for us, a fragrant offering and sacrifice to God." So when Christ died for sinners, it was like a fragrant offering that was very pleasing to God. Now here in 2 Corinthians, Paul is standing in the *place* of Christ as a missionary, and he is suffering *like* Christ in the service of his conquering Lord, and he says, "We are the aroma of Christ to God." In other words, when we suffer as missionaries in the service of Christ, it's like Christ suffering for the lost, and God smells this fragrance of sacrificial love, and it pleases him.

Broken Heart, Joyful Heart

That's the picture so far. But then comes the heart-rejoicing and heartbreaking parts of missionary service. This aroma of the love of Christ in the sacrificial service of the missionary may please God, but it does not please everybody. This aroma divides the world: "For we are the aroma of Christ to God among those who are being saved and among those who are perishing, to one a fragrance from death to death, to the other a fragrance from life to life" (2 Corinthians 2:15–16).

Some people smell the sacrificial love of Christ in the life of a missionary, and it smells only like death. They hear the gospel, and all they hear is death. They look at the cross, and all they see is death. They see no life, no hope, no future, no joy, so they turn away. And if they turn away forever, they die. They are the perishing. The smell of death leads to death.

That's the heartbreaking side of missions: they are people who don't believe. They don't see Christ as precious, don't see his suffering as a treasure. They don't smell his death for sinners as the sweetest fragrance in the universe. It's not a satisfying fragrance. It's simply the smell of death.

But there is a heart-rejoicing side of missions as well. Those who are being saved smell the death of Christ as the aroma of life (v. 16). They see in his death the substitute that they so desperately need before God. So they don't turn away. They believe him and receive him and embrace him and treasure him and they live—forever. Smelling Christ as the aroma of life gives life.

Those are Paul's two pictures of his life as a missionary. First, God conquered him when he was his enemy. He is now leading Paul both in triumph and in suffering. There is reason to exult in this procession, and there is reason to groan in this procession. Paul's calling is to show the sufferings of Christ to the world in his own suffering. Second, Christ is a sweet-smelling sacrifice to God, and Paul is sharing in Christ's mission and sufferings so that he becomes this very fragrance in the world—a fragrance that some smell as life and live, but others smell as death and die.

Who Is Sufficient for These Things?

Now Paul asks at the end of verse 16—and I make it our closing question—"Who is sufficient for these things?" Who can bear the weight of knowing that the aroma of your Christ-exalting life will lead some to eternal life and others to eternal death? The situation is as serious as if you walked down a busy city street at lunch hour, and some would smile, come in behind you, and be saved, and everyone else would drop dead. Who could bear it? That's what Paul asks.

In one sense, the answer is no one. But that's not Paul's main point. He said in 2 Corinthians 1:12 and Romans 1:5 that he carries out this very ministry by the grace of God. He is not sufficient—and you and I are not sufficient—in ourselves. No missionary feels sufficient. But 2 Corinthians 3:5 says, "Our sufficiency is from God."

So the utterly crucial question for many of you, as you have prayed and thought about giving your life, or a substantial part of it, to missions, is this: *Can I do this? Can I bear this weight of being the aroma of Christ in some new place?* By God's grace, you can.

Five Tests

Paul gives us five tests in verse 17 to help us know the answer to this question. I will turn them into questions for you to answer.

First, do you treasure Christ enough so that you do not peddle his word? Paul says, "For we are not, like so many, peddlers of God's word." That is, these peddlers don't love

Christ. They love money and use Christ. So the first test is: Do you love Christ more than money?

The next four phrases in verse 17 all modify the word *speak*. Paul says that he speaks from sincerity, from God, before God, and in Christ.

So I ask you, second, will you speak from sincerity? Will you be real? Will you mean what you say? Will you renounce all pretense and hypocrisy?

Third, will you speak as from God? That is, will you take not only your commission from God, but your words and your authority from God? Will you speak his words, and not your own? Will you speak in his authority, and not your own? Will you draw your strength and guidance from his power and wisdom, and not your own?

Fourth, will you speak as before God? That is, will you reckon him to be your judge rather than any man? Will you care more about his assessment of your words and not be deterred by human criticism?

Fifth, will you speak as in Christ? That is, will you get your identity and your assurance and your confidence and your hope and your courage from your union with Christ?

There are no perfect missionaries. The answer to these questions should be: *Oh yes, Lord, as much as I know my heart, that is what I intend to be. Help me to love you more than money, to be real and sincere, to speak your word, to fear no man, and to get all I need from Christ.*

ISAIAH 25:1–8

O LORD, you are my God; I will exalt you; I will praise your name, for you have done wonderful things, plans formed of old, faithful and sure. ²For you have made the city a heap, the fortified city a ruin; the foreigners' palace is a city no more; it will never be rebuilt. ³Therefore strong peoples will glorify you; cities of ruthless nations will fear you. ⁴For you have been a stronghold to the poor, a stronghold to the needy in his distress, a shelter from the storm and a shade from the heat; for the breath of the ruthless is like a storm against a wall, ⁵like heat in a dry place. You subdue the noise of the foreigners; as heat by the shade of a cloud, so the song of the ruthless is put down. ⁶On this mountain the LORD of hosts will make for all peoples a feast of rich food, a feast of well-aged wine, of rich food full of marrow, of aged wine well refined. ⁷And he will swallow up on this mountain the covering that is cast over all peoples, the veil that is spread over all nations. ⁸He will swallow up death forever; and the Lord GOD will wipe away tears from all faces, and the reproach of his people he will take away from all the earth, for the LORD has spoken.

8

Cities of Ruthless Nations Will Fear the Lord

What is the greatest blessing that you, or I, or any church planter or missionary, could bring to a people or a city? To be used by God to awaken in them a *passion for the supremacy of God in all things through the redeeming work of Jesus Christ.* There is no greater joy, no more durable joy, than the joy of seeing and savoring and being satisfied in the supremacy of God in all things.

Or to put it another way, there is no greater joy, and therefore no greater blessing, that any city, people group, or person could have, than the joy of seeing, being with, being lovingly enveloped in, and being transformed by the glory of God's infinite supremacy. God is the greatest, most supreme, most beautiful, most powerful, most wise, most just, most loving, most holy, most glorious of all beings. To know him, to be loved by him, to be transformed by him so that we reflect him, to be with him forever is the greatest blessing any person or any people or any city could ever have.

"You make known to me the path of life; in your presence there is fullness of joy; at your right hand are pleasures forevermore" (Psalm 16:11). Fullness of joy—forever. The greatest and the longest joy is in the presence of God, where we see and savor his supremacy, in all things, forever.

God Is the Gospel

The aim of the gospel is to bring people through Jesus Christ to God. "Christ also suffered once for sins, the righteous for the unrighteous, that he might bring us to God" (1 Peter 3:18).

God himself is the ultimate goal of the gospel. The gospel of Christ crucified and risen brings us many good things: forgiveness of sins, imputed righteousness, the removal of God's wrath, escape from hell, the hope of heaven, peace of conscience, and in the end, total healing, with a new body and everlasting freedom from pain. But none of these is the ultimate goal of the gospel. The ultimate goal is God—to be with God, satisfied in God himself. Christ suffered to bring us to God. In his presence is fullness of joy. At his right hand are pleasures forever. Knowing God, being with God, enjoying God—this is the gospel's final blessing. God is the goal of the gospel.

Missions, therefore, is about the greatness of God, the glory of God, the all-satisfying beauty of God. "Christ became a servant," Paul says, "in order that the Gentiles might glorify God for his mercy" (Romans 15:8–9). And God's mercy is most glorified in us when we are most satisfied in it. We glorify God for his mercy by reveling in his mercy, exulting in his mercy, glorying in his mercy, swimming, frolicking, rejoicing in his mercy.

The Challenge Ahead

The problem is that the nations and the peoples and the cities of the world are not moving in this direction. The cities and the peoples of the world who need the blessing of the gospel are not standing on tiptoe, waiting for the message of the humbling of man and the supremacy of God. They are in fact hostile to this message. "The mind that is set on the flesh is hostile to God, for it does not submit to God's law; indeed, it cannot. Those who are in the flesh cannot please God" (Romans 8:7–8).

The peoples we want to bless with an all-satisfying passion for the supremacy of God through Christ are peoples who love their sin. They are strong and, in many cases, ruthless cities. They are not ready to fall into your arms. Your mission will be opposed not only with the natural hostility of the human heart, but with supernatural, demonic power. You will not merely war against human forces of evil, but against mammoth powers of darkness.

So my aim is to encourage you with a vision of stunning hope: our almighty God is on your side, he loves your mission, and he has promised an astonishing triumph in the end. Let's consider Isaiah 25:1–8.

No Light Is Lit in Vain

One indispensable motive for mission is hope—the confidence that we are engaged in a cause that will triumph in the end. No life laid down in the cause of world evangelization is laid down in vain. No dollar given is in vain. No sermon preached is in vain. No prayer offered is in vain. No candle of gospel light is ever lit in vain.

I love Paul's words. I cling to them! "Be steadfast, immovable, always abounding in the work of the Lord, knowing that in the Lord your labor is not in vain" (1 Corinthians 15:58). Our energy and sacrifice and focus are sustained by hope—the confidence that God's kingdom will triumph in this world.

This passage in Isaiah is a picture of that hope. Don't worry that you can't answer all the timing questions and all the detail questions about how the triumph of God will eventually come. This text doesn't answer all our questions about the end. What Old Testament prophets do again and again is give us a picture of the final day of victory—from one angle and then from another angle. Each time the aim is that we take heart, give God the glory, and press on in hope-filled allegiance to Christ and hope-filled missions.

I want to focus our attention for a few minutes on this picture of God's victory, then jump to the New Testament where the power of God begins to triumph in a particular Roman city, and then jump to our churches as support bases for missions around the world.

Seeing with Isaiah

First, let's look at what Isaiah sees. What he sees stretches from eternity past to eternity future. It is a huge vision.

Eternity Past

Look at verse 1: "O Lord, you are my God; I will exalt you; I will praise your name, for you have done wonderful things, *plans formed of old*, faithful and sure." God had made plans long ago in perfect faithfulness. And now he is bringing his plans to pass in working wonders.

God is a planning God. He gives forethought to what he does. He is wise. And because he is all-knowing, he is never playing catch-up. He takes all his knowledge into account in making all his plans. He is never caught off guard. If he wins in the last three seconds of the battle, he planned it that way. God never "gets lucky." Isaiah stresses this in chapter 46: "I am God, and there is no other; I am God, and there is none like me, declaring the end from the beginning and from ancient times things not yet done, saying, 'My counsel shall stand, and I will accomplish all my purpose'" (Isaiah 46:9–10).

Eternity Future

So in verse 1 Isaiah sees a vision of God's plan stretching from eternity past. And now to eternity future. Look at verses 6–8. Robert Burns, the Scottish poet, once said that he could never read these verses, especially verse 8, without tears. They are one of the most remarkable prophecies in all the Old Testament.

> On this mountain the LORD of hosts will make for all peoples [note: *all peoples!*] a feast of rich food, a feast of well-aged wine, of rich food full of marrow, of aged wine well refined. 7 And he will swallow up on this mountain the covering that is cast over all peoples, the veil that is spread over all nations. 8 He will swallow up death forever; and the Lord GOD will wipe away tears from all faces, and the reproach of his people he will take away from all the earth, for the LORD has spoken.

So Isaiah sees the day coming when all the nations—

representatives from all the people groups (Revelation 5:9)—will no longer be at odds with Yahweh, the God of Israel, and his Messiah, whom we know to be Jesus. They will no longer worship Bel or Nebo or Molech or Allah or Buddha or utopian social programs or capitalistic growth possibilities or ancestors or animistic spirits. Instead, they will come in faith to the banquet on God's mountain. And they will have the veil of sorrow removed, and death shall be swallowed up, and the reproach of God's people will be removed, and tears shall be gone forever.

A Feast for All Peoples

That's the setting for understanding the vision of verse 3, which is the word that I have in mind mainly for your encouragement and hope: "Therefore strong peoples will glorify you; cities of ruthless nations will fear you" (Isaiah 25:3). In other words, God is stronger than the strong peoples, and he is so powerful and so gracious that in the end he will turn cities of ruthless nations to fear him.

This is not the cowering fear of enemies. This is the reverential fear of converts. We know this because the subdued peoples of verse 3 are included in the *all peoples* of verse 6: "On this mountain the LORD of hosts will make *for all peoples* a feast of rich food, a feast of well-aged wine, of rich food full of marrow, of aged wine well refined." So the vision of verse 3 is that strong peoples and the cities of these ruthless nations will turn and fear the Lord—their hostility the gospel will be overcome, and they will believe.

The picture Isaiah gives us is one of all nations turned to God in worship, a great banquet for all the peoples, the removal of all suffering and grief and reproach from the nations who have become his people, and the final putting away of death forever. This triumph is sure because God is doing it. As verse 1 says, he planned it long ago and he is working wonders to bring it to pass. Therefore, we can be certain of it.

Not one life spent in the cause of world evangelization is spent in vain. Not one prayer or one dollar or one sermon or one letter of encouragement mailed or one little light shining in some dark place—nothing in the cause of advancing the kingdom is in vain. The triumph is sure.

Paul's Mission Strategy

Now let's look at one New Testament picture of how the cities of ruthless nations would be subdued and come to fear Yahweh.

Ruthless Philippi

Paul's mission strategy was to go from city to city and plant the church. From the city, the surrounding area was then evangelized. For example, in Acts 19:10 Luke says that because of Paul's two-year investment in Ephesus "all the residents of Asia heard the word of the Lord." That was the strategy: bringing the blessing of the gospel of Jesus Christ, the power of God unto salvation, from city to city.

Paul got a vision from Macedonia in northern Greece: "Come over to Macedonia and help us" (Acts 16:9). Paul's response to this was to take his team from Turkey to Macedonia and focus on the first major city, Philippi.

> And when Paul had seen the vision, immediately we sought to go on into Macedonia, concluding that God had called us to preach the gospel to

> them. So, setting sail from Troas, we made a
> direct voyage to Samothrace, and the follow-
> ing day to Neapolis, and from there to Philippi,
> which is a leading city of the district of Mace-
> donia and a Roman colony. We remained in this
> city some days. (Acts 16:10–12)

Philippi was pagan and diverse—you will never plant a
church in a city more alien to Christianity than Philippi
was. There was the imperial cult that deified the Caesar.
There were the Greek gods with their temples and altars
and Latin names: Jupiter, Juno, Minerva, Mars. Artemis
had her cult under the name Bendis. And there were sanc-
tuaries to the gods of Egypt, especially Isis and Serapis, as
well as the Phrygian Cybele known as the great mother
goddess. It was, to use the words of Isaiah, a city of ruthless nations that Paul wanted to see revere God.

The Macedonian Model

So Paul preached by the river, and God saved one woman,
Lydia. He preached in the streets, and God saved a slave
girl who had been possessed by a spirit of fortune telling.
He was arrested with Silas and put in prison, and they
sang down a miracle and preached the gospel to the jailer,
and God saved him and his family. And there was the
church: a businesswoman who sold purple goods, a former
slave girl, and a low-level government employee.

What became of this strategy of blessing the city of
Philippi with a new gospel-driven church? When Paul
wrote to the Philippians years later from prison in Rome,
they were clearly unparalleled in his affections. "And you
Philippians yourselves know that in the beginning of the

gospel, when I left Macedonia, no church entered into partnership with me in giving and receiving, except you only" (Philippians 4:15).

This growing church was the exact opposite of ruthless and cruel and harsh and selfish. They had become so transformed that they were models to the church in Corinth. We see this is 2 Corinthians 8:1–2. "We want you to know, brothers, about the grace of God that has been given among the churches of Macedonia, for in a severe test of affliction, their abundance of joy and their extreme poverty have overflowed in a wealth of generosity on their part."

Archaeologists have uncovered two large basilicas in Philippi from the fifth or sixth century. Thousands from this city of ruthless nations had come to fear the true God.

Torch the Glaciers of Ten Thousand Cities

So take heart. The vision to be a gospel blessing to all the peoples of the world is a biblical vision. And even more wonderful, it is a vision that cannot fail—if any one of us walks away from it, someone else will pick it up. God will see to that. Christ has redeemed a people from every tribe and tongue and people and nation. "Strong peoples will glorify him; and cities of ruthless nations *will* fear the Lord."

If you look out across America and the world and the moral and spiritual climate appears bleak, you are right. There is a great glacier spreading, and the love of many grows cold, and there are heightened hostilities to the gospel. But our job is to torch the glaciers over ten thousand cities. God is with us in this. And he will not fail. So let's plant the flag of Isaiah 25:3 in ten thousand places around this world. Strong peoples *will* glorify him; and cities of ruthless nations *will* fear the Lord.

GALATIANS 2:1-10

Then after fourteen years I went up again to Jerusalem with Barnabas, taking Titus along with me. ²I went up because of a revelation and set before them (though privately before those who seemed influential) the gospel that I proclaim among the Gentiles, in order to make sure I was not running or had not run in vain. ³But even Titus, who was with me, was not forced to be circumcised, though he was a Greek. ⁴Yet because of false brothers secretly brought in—who slipped in to spy out our freedom that we have in Christ Jesus, so that they might bring us into slavery— ⁵to them we did not yield in submission even for a moment, so that the truth of the gospel might be preserved for you. ⁶And from those who seemed to be influential (what they were makes no difference to me; God shows no partiality)— those, I say, who seemed influential added nothing to me. ⁷On the contrary, when they saw that I had been entrusted with the gospel to the uncircumcised, just as Peter had been entrusted with the gospel to the circumcised ⁸(for he who worked through Peter for his apostolic ministry to the circumcised worked also through me for mine to the Gentiles), ⁹and when James and Cephas and John, who seemed to be pillars, perceived the grace that was given to me, they gave the right hand of fellowship to Barnabas and me, that we should go to the Gentiles and they to the circumcised. ¹⁰Only, they asked us to remember the poor, the very thing I was eager to do.

9

Gospel to the Nations, Generosity to the Poor

The first thing I want to do in this chapter is walk from Galatians 1:6 to 2:10 so we can see the flow of Paul's thought. Then we will work our way backward and focus on three parts of this passage: the poor, the gospel, and the call.

Paul's Gospel Is from Christ, Not Man

Paul begins his letter with astonishment. The Galatians are about to abandon the gospel because some professing Christians had come among them preaching the necessity of circumcision for salvation. Salvation by grace alone through faith alone on the basis of Christ alone was at stake, and Paul can hardly believe what he is hearing. He says in 1:6, "I am astonished that you are so quickly deserting him who called you in the grace of Christ and are turning to a different gospel."

Then he tells them there is no other gospel that can save anyone from sin and hell, and if anyone tells you there is, well, consider his words in verse 9: "As we have said before, so now I say again: If anyone is preaching to you a gospel contrary to the one you received, let him be accursed." In street language, but very literally, Paul says, "To hell with him."

He goes on to say that his gospel is truly from Jesus Christ, not from any man or from his own head. In verses 11–12, he says, "For I would have you know, brothers, that the gospel that was preached by me is not man's gospel. For I did not receive it from any man, nor was I taught it, but I received it through a revelation of Jesus Christ."

Then he defends this amazing claim by reminding them how incredibly his life had changed. In verses 13–14 he reminds them what a zealous persecutor of the church he was. Then in verses 15–17 he describes the change in his life, and that it came without going to Jerusalem.

> But when he who had set me apart before I was born, and who called me by his grace, was pleased to reveal his Son to me, in order that I might preach him among the Gentiles, I did not immediately consult with anyone, nor did I go up to Jerusalem to those who were apostles before me, but I went away into Arabia, and returned again to Damascus.

After three years, he made a fifteen-day trip to Jerusalem and met Peter and James, the Lord's brother, and then he disappeared into Syria and Cilicia for fourteen years (vv. 18–22).

Paul's point in documenting all that was to make clear

that his gospel is from Christ and not from man. It's as if he is saying, "I am not a secondhand apostle. My authority and my message are not derivative. They come from the risen Christ, not Peter and James."

Paul's Gospel Matches the Apostles'

But now in chapter 2, he adds an emphasis on the unity he shares with the original twelve apostles. Paul knows that if his gospel and his apostleship are rejected by the original twelve apostles, there would be an intolerable split in the foundation of Christ's church, and he would be running in vain. So he must establish his independence *and* his unity with the original apostles. That unity is the point of 2:1–10.

With Titus in Jerusalem

Paul writes, "Then after fourteen years [a long period that establishes his independence] I went up again to Jerusalem with Barnabas, taking Titus along with me" (v. 1). Taking Titus, an uncircumcised Gentile convert, right into the hotbed of Jewish legal conservatism would function as a test case of his gospel of freedom. Paul goes on: "I went up because of a revelation [Christ told him to go; this is not a human strategy] and set before them (though privately before those who seemed influential) the gospel that I proclaim among the Gentiles, in order to make sure I was not running or had not run in vain" (v. 2).

Things got very tense for a while as the circumcision party—he calls them "false brothers"!—tried to make circumcision necessary for salvation. But Paul did not budge, because the gospel was at stake. This claim regarding circumcision is the "other gospel" that he called damnable in 1:8. He writes,

> But even Titus, who was with me, was not forced to be circumcised, though he was a Greek. Yet because of false brothers secretly brought in—who slipped in to spy out our freedom that we have in Christ Jesus, so that they might bring us into slavery—to them we did not yield in submission even for a moment, so that the truth of the gospel might be preserved for you. (vv. 3–5)

The Right Hand of Fellowship

The next four verses represent one of the most important moments in history—all of history! Unity is reached among the founding apostles of the Christian church, and the gospel is safeguarded from one of its earliest threats. I think it would be fair to say that for the first and greatest missionary to the Gentiles, the most essential thing in missions was to get the gospel right—exactly right. Otherwise he would be running in vain.

In verse 6, Paul continues to stress his independence—that his gospel is from Christ, not man: "And from those who seemed to be influential (what they were makes no difference to me; God shows no partiality)—those, I say, who seemed influential added nothing to me." Then he writes,

> On the contrary, when they saw that I had been entrusted with the gospel to the uncircumcised, just as Peter had been entrusted with the gospel to the circumcised (for he who worked through Peter for his apostolic ministry to the circum-

cised worked also through me for mine to the
Gentiles), and when James and Cephas and John,
who seemed to be pillars, perceived the grace
that was given to me, they gave the right hand of
fellowship to Barnabas and me, that we should
go to the Gentiles and they to the circumcised.
(vv. 7–9).

Then, finally, Paul adds verse 10, showing that he and the
other apostles agreed on one other thing: "Only, they asked
us to remember the poor, the very thing I was eager to do."
Paul agreed with the apostles that concrete financial compassion for the poor was a crucial part of apostolic ministry.

Now let's turn around and go backward through this
text, focusing this time on only three parts: the poor, the
gospel, and the call.

Remember the Poor

First, notice four things about the poor: (1) the apostles
were of one mind about this, (2) it was important enough
to mention alongside the purity of the gospel, (3) Paul
was not just *willing* to do it but *eager* to do it, and (4) the
passion and this priority for the poor came from Christ
himself.

The first three are crystal clear from verse 10: "Only,
they asked us to remember the poor, the very thing I was
eager to do." They are agreed. They mention it explicitly
along with the gospel they share. And Paul's eagerness is
clear: "the very thing I was *eager* to do." Generosity to the
poor was not a burden but a blessing; Paul loved to bless
the poor.

Jesus's Example and Teaching

But where did this passion and this priority come from? For Paul, I think we should say that it flowed out of the heart that the gospel created (2 Corinthians 8:9). A forgiven heart is a compassionate heart. But the original twelve apostles had not only the new heart of compassion, but also memories of the way Jesus himself lived.

They remembered, for example, the vision of the judgment in Matthew 25:35–36, where Jesus says, "I was hungry and you gave me food, I was thirsty and you gave me drink, I was a stranger and you welcomed me, I was naked and you clothed me, I was sick and you visited me, I was in prison and you came to me."

They remembered that when Zacchaeus gave half of his possessions to the poor, Jesus said, "Today salvation has come to this house" (Luke 19:9).

They remembered that the evidence of salvation is practical, financial compassion for the poor. When someone invited Jesus to a feast, he responded, "When you give a feast, invite the poor, the crippled, the lame, the blind, and you will be blessed, because they cannot repay you. For you will be repaid at the resurrection of the just" (Luke 14:13–14). And at the inauguration of Jesus's ministry, he said, "The Spirit of the Lord is upon me, because he has anointed me to proclaim good news to the poor" (Luke 4:18).

And so many more places could be cited. The point is that the apostles were agreed on the importance of ministry to the poor because it flows from the center of the gospel—the cross—and because Jesus lived it out. The apostles were eager to bless the poor. It was part of their foundational ministry. I assume, therefore, that it should be a crucial commitment in the church today—in missions and in the ongoing ministry of the church.

Not Just the Christian Poor

And it isn't just the Christian poor. Galatians 6:10 says, "So then, as we have opportunity, let us do good to everyone, and especially to those who are of the household of faith." So yes, take care of your own. But the heart of Christ does not neglect unbelievers.

Paul said in Romans 12:20, "If your enemy is hungry, feed him; if he is thirsty, give him something to drink." Christians who have the heart of Christ and who follow in the paths of the apostles remember both the Christian and the non-Christian poor, and they do as much good for them as they can.

Guard the Gospel

Now let's take our second step backward through the text to the centrality and purity of the gospel in verse 5: "To them [those who were insisting on circumcision for salvation] we did not yield in submission even for a moment, so that the truth of the gospel might be preserved for you."

How attractive it may seem at times—especially in missions—to alter the gospel and make it fit the situation so as not to offend anyone. But Paul doesn't do that. The cultural and religious expectations of many Jewish Christians was that circumcision was necessary. Can't Paul concede that for the sake of peace? And not only did Paul refuse to submit "even for a moment," he says, but he even called them "false brothers" (2:4, 5). Those are really strong words. One slight adjustment to justification by faith alone, and Paul calls the change damnable (1:8), the people "false brothers."

What gospel missionaries take to the nations is really important. Let missionaries be utterly clear about what the gospel is! Let none of them say that doctrine doesn't matter. Let none say that small changes to the gospel can't hurt anybody. May every missionary under pressure to compromise the gospel say with the apostle Paul, "We did not yield in submission even for a moment, so that the truth of the gospel might be preserved for you" (v. 5). This is tough love at home for the sake of the nations.

And that includes the poor. May every missionary to the poor say with Jesus and the apostle Paul, "The Spirit of the Lord is upon me, because he has anointed me to *proclaim good news* to the poor" (Luke 4:18)—the real good news of justification by grace alone, through faith alone, on the basis of Christ's blood and righteousness alone, to the glory of God alone—the good news worth dying for.

Called to Preach Christ

Finally, take a third step backward in the text to look at Paul's call—and ponder your own.

The great gospel promise and hope is Romans 10:13: "Everyone who calls on the name of the Lord will be saved." That promise is true in a jail at midnight in Philippi, where a Gentile jailer listens to two Jews singing in their chains (Acts 16:25–34). It's true in the inner-city projects of Bangkok. It's true in the rubble of Pakistani mountains and in Guatemalan villages. It's true among Somali refugees in Minneapolis.

It's true in Mexico and Kazakhstan and Kenya

and Cameroon and Russia and Papua New Guinea and
the Philippines and Senegal and Japan and Bosnia and
Germany and Ethiopia and Peru and Bolivia and Ecuador
and Brazil and the Czech Republic and Austria and Syria
and the Ivory Coast and Turkey and China and Oman and
the United Arab Emirates and England and Uzbekistan
and Indonesia and India and Zambia. The gospel of Jesus
Christ, the Son of God, saves all who call upon him in
truth.

How God Calls

But Paul goes on to ask in Romans 10,

> How then will they call on him in whom they
> have not believed? And how are they to believe
> in him of whom they have never heard? And
> how are they to hear without someone preach-
> ing? And how are they to preach unless they are
> sent? As it is written, "How beautiful are the feet
> of those who preach the good news!" (vv. 14–15)

This is what God did for Paul. He called him and sent him.
Look at what happened to Paul in Galatians 1:15–16: "But
when he who had set me apart before I was born, and who
called me by his grace, was pleased to reveal his Son to me,
in order that I might preach him among the Gentiles ..."

Notice how Paul says it: "God revealed his Son to me
in order that I might preach him." The way Paul met Jesus
and knew Jesus became his call to be a missionary. God
revealed his Son to Paul, and the effect was that he became
a missionary. He crossed cultures from Pharisaic Judaism
to all the forms of Gentile uncleanness in the Roman
world.

To the Unreached and the Poor

God still calls people today—in a thousand different ways. He has his ways of stirring us to the point where we know we must move, we must venture, we must go toward the unreached and toward the poor. And these two groups of people are almost the same now. Eighty-five percent of the poorest of the poor live in the 10/40 window (from West Africa to the Pacific Rim, ten degrees north to forty degrees north). And ninety-five percent of the least-reached peoples live in the 10/40 window. Globally speaking, the most unreached peoples and the poorest peoples are almost the same; therefore, a call to the unreached peoples is almost the same as a call to the poorest of the poor.

Oh, that God might raise up more and more from among us to go! It will mean a love for the poor and a trust in the gospel and a sense of God's leading and God's provision.

MATTHEW 10:16-31

Behold, I am sending you out as sheep in the midst of wolves, so be wise as serpents and innocent as doves. [17]Beware of men, for they will deliver you over to courts and flog you in their synagogues, [18]and you will be dragged before governors and kings for my sake, to bear witness before them and the Gentiles. [19]When they deliver you over, do not be anxious how you are to speak or what you are to say, for what you are to say will be given to you in that hour. [20]For it is not you who speak, but the Spirit of your Father speaking through you. [21]Brother will deliver brother over to death, and the father his child, and children will rise against parents and have them put to death, [22]and you will be hated by all for my name's sake. But the one who endures to the end will be saved. [23]When they persecute you in one town, flee to the next, for truly, I say to you, you will not have gone through all the towns of Israel before the Son of Man comes. [24]A disciple is not above his teacher, nor a servant above his master. [25]It is enough for the disciple to be like his teacher, and the servant like his master. If they have called the master of the house Beelzebul, how much more will they malign those of his household. [26]So have no fear of them, for nothing is covered that will not be revealed, or hidden that will not be known. [27]What I tell you in the dark, say in the light, and what you hear whispered, proclaim on the housetop [28]And do not fear those who kill the body but cannot kill the soul. Rather fear him who can destroy both soul and body in hell. [29]Are not two sparrows sold for a penny? And not one of them will fall to the ground apart from your Father. [30]But even the hairs of your head are all numbered. [31]Fear not, therefore; you are of more value than many sparrows.

10

"I Am Sending You Out as Sheep in the Midst of Wolves"

When Jesus had finished his great saving work, and had laid down his life to save millions and millions of people who would believe in him, and had risen from the dead, he gave a final mandate to his disciples.

> All authority in heaven and on earth has been given to me. Go therefore and make disciples of all nations, baptizing them in the name of the Father and of the Son and of the Holy Spirit, teaching them to observe all that I have commanded you. And behold, I am with you always, to the end of the age. (Matthew 28:18–20)

That mandate is as valid today as the promise that supports it: "Behold, I am with you always, to the end of the age." If the promise is valid today, then the mandate is valid today. And the promise is valid because it lasts, Jesus said, "to the end of the age." Until Jesus returns, the promise holds that he will be with us. That promise is the basis of the mandate, and so the mandate holds today. Jesus is commanding us, "Go make disciples of all nations."

The Apostle Paul's Ambition

The apostle Paul is the most prominent missionary in the New Testament. He gave his life in obedience to Jesus's mandate. He said in Romans 15:20–21, "I make it my ambition to preach the gospel, not where Christ has already been named, lest I build on someone else's foundation, but as it is written, 'Those who have never been told of him will see, and those who have never heard will understand.'"

This is the difference between a local evangelist and a frontier missionary. Paul said to Timothy, "Do the work of an evangelist" (2 Timothy 4:5). That means, "As the pastor of a local church in a place where the gospel has already taken root, keep on winning people to Jesus. They may know about Christianity and live near lots of Christians there in Ephesus, but keep on evangelizing them. Tell them the gospel. Show them love. Keep on trying to win them." That's local evangelism, and all of us should be a part of it.

But this is not what we mean by *frontier missions*. Frontier missions is what Paul did: "I make it my ambition to preach the gospel, not where Christ has already been named, lest I build on someone else's foundation." Frontier missions is crossing a culture to plant the church where the gospel has not already taken root. This is the mandate that is still valid for us today. The job is not done. And the word of our risen King Jesus is as binding on us today as much as when he first gave it.

This is why we speak of unreached people groups. Jesus gave the mandate to us to make disciples of all these groups, and Paul modeled what frontier missions looks like, making it his ambition to proclaim the gospel where the church was not already planted. Today, the mandate holds: "Make disciples of all nations" (Matthew 28:19). The promise holds: "I am with you always, to the end of the age" (Matthew 28:20). And the stakes are eternal: "Whoever believes in the Son has eternal life; whoever does not obey the Son shall not see life, but the wrath of God remains on him" (John 3:36).

Who Will Go?

So the question is, Who will go? Who will proclaim the gospel of Jesus Christ where the church is not yet planted and flourishing? Should I go? I ask myself this at least once a year. And I mean it seriously. I am willing to go. I think every follower of Jesus is bound by the cords of love and obedience to say, "I am willing to follow you wherever you lead me." Every believer in Jesus should say, "Here am I, send me, if that is your will."

It is not the Lord's will that all his followers be frontier missionaries. But some he calls. How he does it is a wonderful and mysterious thing. No one can explain how the work of God in your life rises to the level of a compelling call to missions. This is the work of the Holy Spirit, and it is marvelous and unfathomable in our eyes. But we know from Scripture, and from church history and experience, that one instrument God uses to awaken a compelling call to missions is the preaching of the word of God—specifically the preaching of passages of Scripture that describe the mandate and its costs and blessings.

The Coming of the Son of Man

In Matthew 10:16–33, Jesus is telling his disciples what it will cost to bear faithful witness and make disciples in the coming years, and what blessings they can count on to sustain them. The text relates directly to the next forty years after he departs, but it is true in principle for the rest of the age. He says in verse 23, "When they persecute you in one town, flee to the next, for truly, I say to you, you will not have gone through all the towns of Israel before the Son of Man comes." I don't understand the coming of the Son of Man in this verse as the second coming of Christ. If it were, this text would be false.

Just like the New Testament speaks of the coming of the kingdom of God in several stages and manifestations, it also helps to think of the coming of the Son of Man in several stages and manifestations. He came to earth the first time and died, he came as the risen Christ from the dead, he came in judgment through the Roman army's destruction of Jerusalem in AD 70, he has come in power from time to time in great awakenings, and he will come in visible bodily form at the end of the age.

So I take Matthew 10:23 to probably refer to the Son of Man's coming in judgment in AD 70. But the fact that this passage refers directly to the work of spreading the gospel to unreached people between AD 30 and 70 does not mean it is irrelevant for us. What Jesus says about the costs and the blessings of the missionary mandate in this passage is true today. And his main point is crystal clear: be a fearless witness in the face of danger. My prayer is that the Holy Spirit would use it to awaken or confirm his calling on your life.

This text powerfully speaks for itself. So let me, without too much comment, focus our attention on six costs and ten blessings of being on the front line of frontier missions.

Six Costs of Frontier Missions

Consider first the costs. These difficulties are the kinds of things we may expect today, even if, in God's forbearance, we may be spared some of them.

1. The Cost of Being Arrested by Authorities

> *Behold, I am sending you out as sheep in the midst of wolves, so be wise as serpents and innocent as doves. Beware of men, for they will deliver you over to courts and flog you in their synagogues, and you will be dragged before governors and kings for my sake, to bear witness before them and the Gentiles. (vv. 16–18)*

When Jesus sends us to bear witness to him in the world, he does not send us out dominant and strong, but weak and seemingly defenseless in ourselves. He sends us as sheep in the midst of wolves, and he expects that at times we will be treated the way wolves treat sheep.

2. The Cost of Family Betrayal

> *Brother will deliver brother over to death, and the father his child, and children will rise against parents and have them put to death. (v. 21)*

This is almost unbelievable: fathers and children will be

so opposed to the Christian faith that they will want each other dead rather than believing.

3. The Cost of Being Hated by All

You will be hated by all for my name's sake. (v. 22)

Be careful that you don't elevate friendship evangelism to the point where this text makes evangelism impossible. "You will be hated by all" does not mean, "You can't do evangelism."

4. The Cost of Being Persecuted and Driven out of Town

When they persecute you in one town, flee to the next. (v. 23)

So yes, go among wolves and be vulnerable as you preach the gospel, but when they lunge at you, step aside. When they open their mouths, don't jump in.

5. The Cost of Being Maligned

If they have called the master of the house Beelze-bul, how much more will they malign those of his household. (v. 25)

Jesus died in our place so that we might escape the wrath of God, not the wrath of man. He was called to suffer for the sake of propitiation; we are called to suffer for the sake of propagation.

6. The Cost of Being Killed

> *Do not fear those who kill the body but cannot kill*
> *the soul. (v. 28)*

They can kill the body. And sometimes they do. Don't ever elevate safety in missions to the point where you assume we have made a mistake if one of our missionaries is killed. Jesus said plainly in Luke 21:16, "Some of you they will put to death."

Ten Blessings of Frontier Missions

For two thousand years, thousands of missionaries— unnamed people of whom the world is not worthy—have counted this cost and put their lives at risk to reach the lost with the only message of salvation in the world. And the reason they could do this is because the blessings so outweigh the costs. May the Lord make these ten blessings that I am about to name overcome all your fears and give you a passion to know him like this.

1. The Blessing of Being Sent by Christ

> *Behold, I am sending you out as sheep in the midst of*
> *wolves, so be wise as serpents and innocent as doves.*
> *(v. 16)*

"I am sending you out." It is a deeply satisfying thing to be sent by the living Christ into his work.

2. The Blessing of Being Given Words by the Spirit of God

> *When they deliver you over, do not be anxious how you are to speak or what you are to say, for what you are to say will be given to you in that hour. For it is not you who speak, but the Spirit of your Father speaking through you. (vv. 19–20)*

What a wonderful thing it is to sense the presence and power of the Spirit in your life, giving you the words you need.

3. The Blessing of Experiencing God's Fatherly Care

> *It is not you who speak, but the Spirit of your Father speaking through you. (v. 20)*

Jesus makes explicit that the one caring for you is your Father in heaven. You may have to leave your father and mother to be a missionary. But you will always have a Father who cares for you.

4. The Blessing of Salvation at the End of It All

> *The one who endures to the end will be saved. (v. 22)*

When all the costs have been paid, you will have the great end of salvation. You will be raised from the dead with no sorrow or pain or sin, and you will see Christ and enter in to his joy, and despite all your imperfections you will hear the words, "Well done."

5. The Blessing of Knowing the Son of Man Is Coming in Judgment and Mercy

You will not have gone through all the towns of Israel before the Son of Man comes. (v. 23)

This was a great encouragement to those persecuted disciples. Jesus comes at just the right time in historical judgments and deliverances, and he will come at the last day and vindicate all his people.

6. The Blessing of Belonging to Jesus's Household

If they have called the master of the house Beelzebul, how much more will they malign those of his household. (v. 25)

Whatever rejection you may experience, Jesus wants you to be sure you are ever aware: This rejection is a sign that you are his. You are part of his household.

7. The Blessing of Knowing That the Truth Will Triumph

Have no fear of them, for nothing is covered that will not be revealed, or hidden that will not be known. (v. 26)

Nothing is hidden that will not be known. For a season in this world, people will mock your proclamation of the truth. They will say, "What is truth?!" But know this, and hold fast to this blessing: The truth will be known. Your proclamation will be vindicated. "Nothing is covered that will not be revealed, or hidden that will not be known."

Count on it. What is scoffed at now will be written across the sky someday. And one minute of that vindication before all your enemies will make every act of patient endurance worthwhile.

8. The Blessing of Having an Immortal Soul

Do not fear those who kill the body but cannot kill the soul. (v. 28)

The soul of the Christian is indestructible. "Truly, truly, I say to you, whoever hears my word and believes him who sent me has eternal life. He does not come into judgment, but has passed from death to life" (John 5:24).

You have already passed from death to life. Henry Martyn, the missionary to Persia, said that he was immortal until his work on earth was done. True. And he would have also agreed that in the fuller sense: you are immortal after your work on earth is done. That is Jesus's point here.

9. The Blessing of Having a Father Who Sovereignly Rules the Details of Your Life

Are not two sparrows sold for a penny? And not one of them will fall to the ground apart from your Father. (v. 29)

Jesus mentions the fall of a sparrow to the ground because nothing seems more insignificant than that. Yet God, your Father, oversees that and governs that. So you may always know that your Father, who loves you as his precious child, oversees and governs every detail of your life.

10. The Blessing of Being Valued by God

Fear not, therefore; you are of more value than many sparrows. (v. 31)

God does not despise his children. He values his children. He values you, first, because by your union with Jesus Christ, all of his perfection is imputed to you. He values you, second, because by the Spirit, you are being changed from one degree of glory to the next, and God loves the sanctifying work of his own hands. He delights in what you are becoming.

God's Call to the Frontier

How does God call people to give their lives in missions? He does it, along with other influences, by the mysterious and wonderful awakening of fear-conquering desire for the work through the preaching of his word. He does it by helping us count the costs so there is no romantic naiveté about missions. And he does it by filling us with a longing to know these blessings to the full.

For many of you, God has been doing this for some time now, and this chapter is a seal to what has already been done. For others of you, this chapter has awakened a new sense of calling, and you really believe God is stirring you to go. May the Lord confirm his work in your life.

PSALM 96

Oh sing to the Lord a new song;
sing to the Lord, all the earth!
²Sing to the Lord, bless his name;
tell of his salvation from day to day.
³Declare his glory among the nations,
his marvelous works among all the peoples!
⁴For great is the Lord, and greatly to be praised;
he is to be feared above all gods.
⁵For all the gods of the peoples are worthless idols,
but the Lord made the heavens.
⁶Splendor and majesty are before him;
strength and beauty are in his sanctuary.

⁷Ascribe to the Lord, O families of the peoples,
ascribe to the Lord glory and strength!
⁸Ascribe to the Lord the glory due his name;
bring an offering, and come into his courts!
⁹Worship the Lord in the splendor of holiness;
tremble before him, all the earth!

¹⁰Say among the nations, "The Lord reigns!
Yes, the world is established; it shall never be moved;
he will judge the peoples with equity."

¹¹Let the heavens be glad, and let the earth rejoice;
let the sea roar, and all that fills it;
¹²let the field exult, and everything in it!
Then shall all the trees of the forest sing for joy
¹³before the Lord, for he comes,
for he comes to judge the earth.
He will judge the world in righteousness,
and the peoples in his faithfulness

11

Music and Missions for the Glory of God

The Psalms aim to shape our thinking and our feeling. Psalm 42, for example, teaches us how to be discouraged well. Psalm 51 shows us how to be brokenhearted well by guilt and regret. Psalm 103 displays the essential importance of continually expressing gratitude and praise and blessing to the Lord. And Psalm 69 helps us to rightly endure opposition, mistreatment, and injustice. But where do the Psalms ultimately take us?

The key and goal of the Psalms, at every point, is Jesus Christ exalted among all the peoples. No portion of the Psalms—no portion of Scripture—is complete without him, and neither is this book. That is why, in this chapter, we join the author of Psalm 96 in extolling and glorifying God as sovereign Creator, Savior, and Judge. For the Psalms ultimately take us to the ends of the earth, with a song on our lips, until the day our Savior returns and receives his kingship among all nations.

Singing and the Nations

Singing and nations—music and missions—for the glory
of God: these are what stand out to me from Psalm 96.
How shall we think and feel with God about the nations
and about singing and about the glory of the coming
King? How are they related in this psalm and in the age to
come? And how are they related to Jesus?

God did not make known his ways or reveal his glory
or display his marvelous works for you alone, or for your
ethnic group alone. He did it with a view to the nations—
all the nations. This passage is not referring to political
states, but nations, what the psalm calls *peoples*, be they
Korean or Kurdish, Somali or Sioux, Irish or Italian. Trace
with me the focus on the nations in this psalm. The psalmist says that God's people should do at least three things
for the nations: *declare* God's glory, *summon* them to join in,
and *warn* them of judgment should they fail to do so.

Declare, Summon, Warn

First, we should declare to the nations the truth about
God's glory and works and salvation. "Sing to the Lord,
bless his name; tell of his salvation from day to day.
Declare his glory among the nations, his marvelous works
among all the peoples!" (vv. 2–3). Tell of his salvation,
declare his glory, declare his marvelous works. Do this
"among the nations." Do this "among *all* the peoples." All
of them. Leave none out. And then, in keeping with verse
10, sum up your declaration with the message of the kingship of God over the nations: "Say among the nations, 'The
Lord reigns!'"

Second, we should summon the nations to join us, the people of God, in ascribing glory to him and singing praise to him. "Ascribe to the Lord, O families of the peoples, ascribe to the Lord glory and strength!" (v. 7). "Sing to the Lord, all the earth!" (v. 1). Don't just tell the earth facts about the greatness and the glory of God—bid them to join you in praising him. Call for their conversion. All the nations must bow before the one true God of Israel, whom we know now as the Father of our Lord Jesus the Messiah.

Third, let's not merely declare God's glory to the nations, or merely summon them to join us in ascribing glory to him. Let us also warn them of the reason for this declaration and summons: because they are depending on false gods, and judgment is coming on all the nations.

> All the gods of the peoples are worthless idols,
> but the Lord made the heavens. (v. 5)

> Yes, the world is established; it shall never be
> moved; he will judge the peoples with equity. (v. 10)

> He comes, for he comes to judge the earth. He
> will judge the world in righteousness, and the
> peoples in his faithfulness. (v. 13)

In other words, when the psalmist says, "sing to the Lord, *all* the earth" (v. 1), and "declare … his marvelous works among *all* the peoples" (v. 3), and "he is to be feared above *all* gods" (v. 4), and "tremble before him, *all* the earth" (v. 9), and "*all* the gods of the peoples are worthless idols" (v. 5), he really means *all*. The God of the Psalms lays claim on the allegiance of every people—all of them, in all their unimaginable diversity of culture and religion.

Missions: Glorious Call to the Nations

Do not, the psalm implies, leave out any nation, any people, or any family—all of them must convert to the true and living God and abandon all their other gods. Do not let any unloving trend of multiculturalism make you shrink back from the loving work of calling every people from every other religion to repent and ascribe all glory to the one and only true and living God.

Consider this passage from the New Testament, in which I have replaced *Gentiles* with the equivalent term *nations*.

> "I will praise you among the [nations], and sing to your name." And again it is said, "Rejoice, O [nations], with his people." And again, "Praise the Lord, all you [nations], and let all the peoples extol him." And again Isaiah says, "The root of Jesse will come, even he who arises to rule the [nations]; in him will the [nations] hope." (Romans 15:9–12)

These quotes are from the Psalms, Deuteronomy, and Isaiah. Paul the apostle piles them up, one after another, to support the coming of Jesus as the Messiah *for all nations*. That's especially clear from the two preceding verses: "I tell you that Christ became a servant to the circumcised [the Jews] to show God's truthfulness, in order to confirm the promises given to the patriarchs, and in order that the Gentiles [the nations] might glorify God for his mercy. As it is written …" (Romans 15:8–9). Then come the Old Testament promises summoning all the nations to praise God for his mercy—for the work of Jesus Christ on the cross in dying for sinners, thus making mercy possible for rebel Gentile sinners like us.

How should you and I feel about this emphasis, across the Old and New Testaments, on all the nations and all the peoples? God is not telling us this so that we feel exhausted, but rather that we feel exhilarated. And this encouragement is for both missionary *goers* and missionary *senders*—all of us who believe in the one true God, revealed most fully in the God-man, Jesus Christ.

Why do I say this? Look at verse 1 of Psalm 96, where the missionary impulse to all the nations flows *from* singing and calls *for* singing: "Oh sing to the Lord a new song; sing to the Lord, all the earth!" This is a singing mission, an exhilarating mission. This is the way you feel when your team has won the crosstown rivalry or the Super Bowl or the World Cup—only a thousand times greater.

"Declare his glory among the nations, his marvelous works among all the peoples!" (v. 3). We are speaking of *glory*. We are speaking of marvelous works, not boring works or ordinary works. We have tasted and seen that this God is greater to know than all other greatness. "Great is the Lord, and greatly to be praised" (v. 4). We are thrilled and exhilarated to know him and sing to him, and we summon the world—*all* the peoples—to sing with us to him.

Largest Cause of All

If you are one who can say from the heart, "Jesus is Lord," then you were made for this. When you confess Jesus

as the Lord of the universe, you sign up for significance
beyond all your dreams. Whether you're a businessman, a
homemaker, or a student, to belong to Jesus means that
you must embrace the nations for which he died and
over which he will rule. Your heart was made for this, and
until you embrace this global calling there will always be
a measure of sickness in your soul—a partial emptiness
where God's passion for his glory among the nations
belongs.

In the early 1900s, the Laymen's Missionary Movement was born among businessmen who were captured
by a holy ambition to get behind what God was doing in
the massive Student Volunteer Movement. Here is what
J. Campbell White, the first secretary of the Laymen's
Missionary Movement, wrote.

> Most men are not satisfied with the permanent
> output of their lives. Nothing can wholly satisfy
> the life of Christ within his followers except the
> adoption of Christ's purpose toward the world
> he came to redeem. Fame, pleasure, and riches
> are but husks and ashes in contrast with the
> boundless and abiding joy of working with God
> for the fulfillment of his eternal plans. The men
> who are putting everything into Christ's under-
> taking are getting out of life its sweetest and
> most priceless rewards. [9]

How should you feel about the global purpose of Jesus
Christ to be glorified among all the nations? You should

---

9. J. Campbell White, "The Laymen's Missionary Movement," in *Perspectives on the World Christian Movement*, ed. Ralph D. Winter and Stephen C. Hawthorne (Pasadena, CA: William Carey Library, 1981), 225.

feel like this cause is the consummation of your significance in life. Many other things are important, but this is the largest cause of all. Every consistent follower of the Lord of lords and King of kings embraces this purpose. Every healthy Christian finds the consummation of his existence in being a part of this great purpose—that God be glorified among all the nations.

How Should We Feel about the Nations?

What is the situation among the nations today? Stunning shifts are taking place as God gathers his elect *from* all the nations and sends his church *to* all the nations—indeed from everywhere to everywhere. Europe and America are no longer the center of gravity in world Christianity. The center is shifting south and east. Latin America, Africa, and Asia are experiencing phenomenal growth and are becoming the great sending churches.[10]

Organizations such as Joshua Project and People Groups are showing us who the nations actually are—how many such groups there are and how reached or unreached with the gospel they are. As of this writing, Joshua Project says that there are nearly eight thousand "unreached" or "minimally reached" people groups (both categories are defined in part as having an evangelical population of less than two percent). Together, these two groups compose a shocking 45.3 percent of the world population.

I thank God that there are people doing this diffi-

---

10. See, for example, Philip Jenkins's books *The Next Christendom* and *The New Faces of Christianity*.

cult research to help us understand the task that remains
before us. Go to these websites, and start learning about
the global situation.[11] And then dream about how your life,
whether as goer or sender, might be more fully involved in
declaring God's glory among the nations—his marvelous
works among all the peoples.

How should you feel about the nations of the world?
You should have a passion for their salvation. You should
be thrilled that God rules over them all and calls us to be
his emissaries to them all, with the best news in the world.
You should be exhilarated that God will have a people of
his own from all the nations, singing to him and ascribing
glory and strength to his Son.

You were made for this kind of joy. All the other joys
of the Psalms, all the other emotions of the Psalms, are
taking us here: the glory of God celebrated and sung by all
the peoples of the earth.

Music: Striking the Singing Note

As we have already glimpsed, flying like a banner over all
the emphasis on the nations in Psalm 96 are verses 1 and
2, and they are all about singing. "Oh sing to the Lord a
new song; sing to the Lord, all the earth! Sing to the Lord,
bless his name; tell of his salvation from day to day." Why
would you begin such a psalm—about the global reach
of God's kingdom and the duty to "tell of his salvation
from day to day" (v. 2) and to "declare his glory among the
nations" (v. 3)—with the command to sing to the Lord?

The answer is simple: you can't summon the nations

---

11. *JoshuaProject.net* and *www.PeopleGroups.org*

to sing if *you* are not singing. And we *are* summoning the nations—all the nations—to sing to the Savior and Judge of all the earth. Our goal is not mere belief or mere behavior changes. Our goal is wholehearted, whole-minded, whole-souled joy in God that overflows in song. "Let the nations be glad and sing for joy" (Psalm 67:4).

New Song in Our Day

But why *new* songs? Notice that these new songs are *to* the Lord and not just *about* the Lord. "Oh sing *to the* Lord a new song; sing *to the* Lord, all the earth!" (v. 1). It's not wrong to sing about the Lord. The Psalms do it all the time. But when new songs are being written and sung "to the Lord," something is happening in the church. It's a sign of unusual life and vibrancy. People are not just living off the spiritual capital of previous generations, but they are dealing vibrantly with the living God and their songs are being sung *to* him. He is real. He is personal. He is known. He is precious. He is present. And when these songs are beautiful and biblical and engaging, worship is often more intense and more personal.

That is what the psalm calls for, and that is what has been happening during my entire adult life. Around the world there is a new song and a new vibrancy and a new personal engagement in singing to the Lord. And the astonishing thing in our time is the way this awakening of singing to the Lord with new songs has such a strong global and missionary flavor.

To my knowledge, singing has never been more at the forefront of missions than it is today. God is doing something wonderful in the fulfillment of Psalm 96. It is far bigger than any one denomination, any one mission, any one ethnic group, or any one region of the world. The global church is singing—singing to the Lord, singing new songs, and singing about God's lordship over the nations.

Center of Our Singing

Psalm 96 is calling us to spread a passion for the glory of God in all things for the joy of all peoples. And it is calling us to summon these peoples to ascribe glory to God through song. This is both the hardest and the happiest business in the world. Don't miss what God is doing. Be a part of it. Get the nations on your heart. Think rightly about God's global purposes. Feel deeply about his marvelous works. Sing with all your heart to the Lord. Be a part of summoning the nations to join you. And may the center of our singing be the same as the center of the new song we will sing in the age to come—namely, the song of the Lamb who was slain.

> And they sang a new song, saying, "Worthy are you to take the scroll and to open its seals, for you were slain, and by your blood you ransomed people for God from every tribe and language and people and nation, and you have made them a kingdom and priests to our God, and they shall reign on the earth." (Revelation 5:9–10)

MATTHEW 28:16-20

Now the eleven disciples went to Galilee, to the mountain to which Jesus had directed them. [17] And when they saw him they worshiped him, but some doubted. [18] And Jesus came and said to them, "All authority in heaven and on earth has been given to me. [19] Go therefore and make disciples of all nations, baptizing them in the name of the Father and of the Son and of the Holy Spirit, [20] teaching them to observe all that I have commanded you. And behold, I am with you always, to the end of the age."

12

Missions Exists Because Worship Doesn't

In 1890, Bethlehem Baptist Church—at that time a twenty-nine-year-old Swedish Baptist Church—sent members Mini and Ola Hanson to an unreached people group in Burma called the Kachin. These people were known as vengeful, cruel, and treacherous. The King of Burma declared to the Hansons when they got there, "So, you are to teach the Kachins! Do you see my dogs over there? I tell you, it will be easier to convert and teach these dogs. You are wasting your life."

The Kachin were completely illiterate, with no written language. Over the next thirty years, Ola Hanson identified and documented 25,000 of their words and published a Kachin-English dictionary. In 1911, he finished translating the New Testament into Kachin. On August 11, 1926, he completed the Old Testament.

In a letter dated August 14 of that year, Hanson wrote, "It is with heartfelt gratitude that I lay this work at the feet of my Master. Pray with us, that our divine Master may bless this work to the salvation of the whole Kachin race." Today, virtually all Kachin can read and write in their own language, as well as Burmese, the national language. And there are more than half a million Kachin Christians.

Holding the Rope for 130 Years

It has been one of the highest privileges of my life to be part of the effort to sustain and grow the legacy of missions at Bethlehem Baptist Church, a legacy that is at this point nearly 130 years in the making. While pastoring there, I often thought, *O Lord, if we falter as a church, if we stumble, if we drop the ropes, so many missionaries will fall.* For we had hundreds of global partners who had gone down into the mines on ropes held by the church. (This is still true at Bethlehem).

"Holding the rope" has long been a powerful image for missions work. It comes from William Carey, who blazed the trail to India in 1792 and saw his mission as that of a miner penetrating into a deep mine—one which had never been explored, and with no one to guide. He said to Andrew Fuller and John Ryland and his other pastor friends, "I will go down, if you will hold the rope." And John Ryland reports, "He took an oath from each of us, at the mouth of the pit, to this effect: that 'while we lived, we should never let go of the rope.'"[12]

We are, all of us who believe, either goers, senders, or disobedient—those who drop into mines, those who hold the ropes, or those who think it's not their business.

---

12. Peter Morden, *Offering Christ to the World* (Waynesboro, GA: Paternoster, 2003), 167.

Rejoice if you are part of a church that doesn't just *support*, but *sends* from your own number, families and singles, to take the gospel to the peoples of the world.

Ten Biblical Convictions Regarding Global Missions

Here are ten biblical convictions that have long driven my commitment to world missions. I pray that they will burn in your soul—for some of you as a God-given compulsion to go, and for others as a God-given compulsion to send.

1. The Fame of God's Name

God is passionately committed to the fame of his name, and that he be worshiped by all the peoples of the world—and this is not egomania; it is love.

Missions, global outreach, is about joining God in his passion to love the nations by offering himself to them for the overflowing joy of their praise.

> Declare his glory among the nations, his marvelous works among all the peoples! (Psalm 96:3)

> Make known his deeds among the peoples, proclaim that his name is exalted. (Isaiah 12:4)

> God sends Jesus on his mission "in order that the Gentiles might glorify God for his mercy." (Romans 15:9)

> He does his mighty works in history "that [his] name might be proclaimed in all the earth." (Romans 9:17)

2. Goal and Fuel of Missions

Therefore, worship is the goal and the fuel of missions; missions exists because worship doesn't.

Missions is a way of saying that *the joy of knowing Christ is not a private or tribal or national or ethnic privilege. It is for all.* And that's why Christians go. Because we have tasted the joy of worshiping Jesus, and we want all the families of the earth included. "All the ends of the earth shall remember and turn to the LORD, and all the families of the nations shall worship before you" (Psalm 22:27).

Seeking the worship of the nations is fueled by the joy of our own worship. You can't commend what you don't cherish. You can't proclaim what you don't prize. Worship is the fuel and the goal of missions.

3. Faith Comes by Hearing

People must be told about Jesus, because there is no salvation and no worship where the gospel of the crucified and risen Son of God is not heard and believed.

There will be no salvation and no true worship among people who have not heard the gospel. Missions is essential for salvation.

> And there is salvation in no one else, for there is no other name under heaven given among men by which we must be saved. (Acts 4:12)

> Faith comes from hearing, and hearing through the word of Christ. (Romans 10:17)

> Whoever has the Son has life; whoever does not have the Son of God does not have life. (1 John 5:12)

Go therefore and make disciples of all nations.
(Matthew 28:19)

4. Worshipers from Every People

God is committed to gathering worshipers from all the
peoples of the world, not just all the countries of the world.

This is what *all nations* means in the Great Commission. Nations like Ojibwe and Fulani and Kachin, not like
the United States and Japan and Argentina. This is what
Jesus bought with his blood. "Worthy are you to take the
scroll and to open its seals, for you were slain, and by your
blood you ransomed people for God from every tribe and
language and people and nation, and you have made them
a kingdom and priests to our God, and they shall reign on
the earth" (Revelation 5:9–10).

The gospel has already reached all the *countries*. But,
according to the Joshua Project, there are nearly eight
thousand unreached or minimally reached *peoples*. That
is why Bethlehem's mission statement says, "We exist to
spread a passion for the supremacy of God in all things for
the joy of all peoples [plural!] through Jesus Christ."

5. Frontier Missionaries

Therefore, there is a critical need for Paul-type missionaries whose calling and passion is to take the gospel to
peoples where there is no access to the gospel at all.

I am distinguishing Paul-type missionaries from
Timothy-type missionaries. Timothy left his home and
served cross-culturally in a city (Ephesus) different from
his own (Lystra). But Paul said in Romans 15:20, "I make
it my ambition to preach the gospel, not where Christ

has already been named." There is still much to do where Christ has been named. But oh how badly we need to pray for an army of hundreds of thousands with Paul's passion to reach the utterly unreached and unengaged peoples of the world.

6. Worthy of God

We must send global partners in a manner worthy of God.

This is why churches have a missions staff and a missions budget and a missions nurture program and support teams for missionaries. "You will do well to send them on their journey in a manner worthy of God" (3 John 6). This is why senders are crucial, along with goers, because not everyone is a frontier missionary. Frontier missionaries cross cultures and plant the church where it's not. But if we are not a goer, there is a great calling: that of sender. And John says we are to do it in a manner worthy of God.

7. Wartime Mindset

It is fitting for us to have a wartime mindset in the use of our resources as long as peoples are without the gospel and we have resources to send it.

In peacetime, the Queen Mary was a luxury liner, but in the Second World War she became a troop carrier. Instead of bunks three-high they were stacked seven-high. Instead of eighteen-piece place settings, there were rations with fork and knife. You allocate your resources differently if it's wartime.

And it *is* wartime. The battles are more constant than in any of our military conflicts, and the losses are eternal.

The Macedonians Paul wrote about are a model for

us in the face of great need. "In a severe test of affliction, their abundance of joy and their extreme poverty have overflowed in a wealth of generosity on their part" (2 Corinthians 8:2). Oh, that we would deepen in our grasp of the urgency of the hour and remember that ultimately we don't own anything. God owns us and all we have. And he cares about how it goes with us in our war effort to reach the nations with the gospel, the gospel that Jesus died to send.

8. Wartime Walkie-Talkie

Prayer is a wartime walkie-talkie, not a domestic intercom.

"I chose you and appointed you," Jesus said, "that you should go and bear fruit … *so that* whatever you ask the Father in my name, he may give it to you" (John 15:16). God has given you a wartime mission: to go and bear fruit. And he gave you prayer for the purpose of accomplishing *that* mission.

One of the reasons our prayer malfunctions is that we try to treat it like a domestic intercom for calling the butler when we want another pillow in the den. But prayer is mainly for those on the front lines of the war effort, so they can call in to headquarters to send help. We are to treat prayer like a battlefield walkie-talkie for calling down the power of the Holy Spirit in the struggle for souls.

9. Suffering Is the Plan

Suffering is not only the price for being in missions; it is God's plan for getting the job done.

This is not just the price many must pay. This is God's strategy for victory.

If they have called the master of the house Beelzebul, how much more will they malign those of
his household. (Matthew 10:25)

They will deliver you up to tribulation and put
you to death, and you will be hated by all nations
for my name's sake. (Matthew 24:9)

Behold, I am sending you out as sheep in the
midst of wolves. (Matthew 10:16)

God's Son won the victory this way. So will we.
"They have conquered him by the blood of the
Lamb and by the word of their testimony, for
they loved not their lives even unto death" (Revelation 12:11).

They *conquered* (not *were conquered*) by testimony and death.

10. The Mission Will Succeed

The global cause of Christ cannot fail, and nothing you do
in this cause is in vain.

Jesus said, "All authority in heaven and on earth
has been given to me. Go therefore and make disciples"
(Matthew 28:18–19). Not some authority—all. He cannot
be defeated.

"I will build my church, and the gates of hell
shall not prevail against it." (Matthew 16:18)

"This gospel of the kingdom will be proclaimed
throughout the whole world as a testimony to all
nations, and then the end will come." (Matthew
24:14)

He has ransomed a people for all the nations. And he will have them.

There are more, but these are ten of the main biblical convictions that can powerfully drive a commitment to global outreach. And for some of you, I pray that as you have been considering these convictions, they have become, again, a confirmation that God is leading you into long-term, cross-cultural missions.

If I Could Start All Over: Six Lessons for Your Twenties

What are the most important things I would do at 22? I'm not thinking in the abstract, but of the real me in 1968. What if I started over with all the same circumstances in place? Well, I would do six things.

1. I would marry a radical, risk-taking, go-anywhere-for-Jesus world-Christian woman.

In fact, I would marry Noël Henry. Not long after we met, when I was 20, I was head over heels in love already. We were talking about marriage three weeks into this relationship, and I said, "If God called me to be a missionary to Africa, would you go?" She said, "Yes, I would see myself called to be by your side—wherever."

We married when I was 22, and my first job was teaching in college, and when I was 33 I felt the irresistible call to be a pastor. And I asked her the morning after that

meeting with God if she would support me in that. And
she said *yes*. One year into that ministry, I was so discouraged. I put my face in my hands at the dining room table.
She was in the bedroom, and I said out loud—pretty seriously—"I think I'm going to Africa." And she didn't miss a
beat from the other room and said, "Tell me when to pack."
This is really significant that you marry the right woman.

We weathered that discouragement, and four years
into that ministry I said to her one day when God had
met us in world missions powerfully at the church, "What
if we invited everybody from the church who is interested
in missions to come over on Friday night? We'll put them
out in the living room and dining room and see if we can
inspire them." And she said, "Sure, let's do that." And one
hundred people showed up.

Twice a year for twenty years, we had one hundred
people in our living room and dining room, and we took
all the furniture and put it upstairs in the bedroom. That's
a lot of work. And women don't like having their houses
intruded upon like that—usually.

The lesson for you: unless you're called to singleness,
pray that your future or present spouse would be a radical,
risk-taking, go-anywhere-for-Jesus world Christian.

2. I would take that young wife of mine and join a Bible-believing, Bible-preaching, Bible-structured, Bible-obedient church.

And I would take her to church every Sunday morning
without fail. And we would throw ourselves into the ministry of that local church in the hope that the community
of believers would care for us, and guard us, and help us

discover our gifts in our early years together, which would then catapult us into a lifetime of ministry.

We joined Lake Avenue Congregational Church in Pasadena, California, when I was 22 and she was 21. Noël discovered a gift for working with mentally disabled adults, and I discovered a teaching gift by teaching seventh-grade boys the first year, ninth-grade boys the second year, and the Galilean adult Sunday school class the third year. The group of deacons there cared for me, and Glenn Dawson laid hold of me, watched over me for three years, sent me to Germany for three years, watched me at Bethel College for a year, brought me back out to Pasadena, and they ordained me seven years later. That's a relationship you cannot overestimate.

The lesson for you: Find a Bible-believing, Bible-preaching, Bible-structured, Bible-obedient church. Join it, serve it, and discover your gifts there. Be accountable to that community as they help you discover and follow God's call on your life.

3. I would go to seminary.

If I were 22 again, I would spend three or four years totally immersed in the most rigorous study of Greek and Hebrew that I could possibly find for a lifetime of fruitful discovery of the glories of Christ in the word of God, in such a way that I would never waiver—no matter what—in my commitment to believe and speak whatever the Bible teaches, wherever God puts me.

I would not prioritize in seminary practical courses, as valuable as those are. But every chance I got, I would prioritize taking exegetical courses because of my conviction at age 72—and I would put it back on that 22-two-year-old—that, in general, practical skills are learned better on the job, in the church, and the deepening and sharpening of exegetical skills for a lifetime of fruitful reading are best accomplished in a rigorous give-and-take classroom setting with the watchful eye of a skilled teacher.

The lesson for you: whether you attend seminary or not, become as Bible-saturated as you can, putting yourself under the influence of the most insightful Bible teachers, both dead and alive.

4. I would resolve to read my Bible every day for the rest of my life.

I would make it more important than eating or getting exercise or kissing my wife. There have been about 18,340 days since I turned 22, and I think I have read my Bible on more of those days than I have eaten. I have certainly read my Bible on more of those days than I have watched television or videos. And I am also certain that I have read my Bible on more of those days than I have kissed my wife because she doesn't go with me on the road, usually. And my Bible does—always does. I never leave my Bible. I might leave my wife for a time, but not my Bible.

I have learned a few things about reading the Bible that I didn't know when I was 22, but if I were, I would resolve

- every day to read my Bible, and not to settle for a hazy, vague awareness of it, but push through the haze to the *wording* itself;
- and I would push into and through the wording of the text itself to the *intention* of the authors—human and divine;

- and I would push through the intention to the *reality* behind the words and the grammar and the logic;
- and I would push into that reality until it was an *emotionally experienced* reality;
- and I would push into and through that emotionally proportional reality until it became *a word and a deed* on my life;
- and I would push through that deed and that word until other people saw the reality and *joined me* in my encounter with God in the Bible.

That's how I would formulate my resolution to read the Bible every day. Nothing is revealed more quickly on the mission field than a superficial encounter with the living God and the glorious realities he has revealed in Scripture. Superficial Bible reading that does not penetrate through the *words* and *intentions* and *reality* and *experience* to *deed* and *life* and an *encounter* with the living God will be of little use on the mission field in the face of massive demonic forces among unreached peoples. You won't survive.

The lesson for you: read your Bible every day. Every day of your life—no exceptions. Never say, "I'll read it if I have time." If you have time for breakfast, you have time for your Bible. Skip breakfast. Don't get your Bible-reading pleasure from the fact that your conscience is clear because you checked the Bible box. Get your pleasure from reading the Bible because of an encounter—a meeting, a fellowship—with the living, supernatural reality that you meet in the Scriptures.

5. I would become a Christian Hedonist.

I would seek to find more joy in God than in anything else in the world for the sake of personal holiness, perseverance through pain, and promotion of the glory of God. That's why I would become a Christian Hedonist. That is, I would get clarity and certainty around the sentence *God is most glorified in you when you are most satisfied in him.* I would nail that sentence, and I would either believe it or not believe it. And if I believed it, I would go for broke in being as satisfied in God as I could possibly be, 24/7, over everything else.

By means of savoring the sweetness of the promises of God in this precious Book, I would put to death every rising quiver of pride, and self-reliance, and lust, and greed, and fear, and, by the power of the Holy Spirit, seek to kill all those sins by the superior pleasure that we have in God. Because unless those sins die, I will be dogged by fruitlessness in this life, and damned in the next.

I would recognize at age 22 that the fight for joy in God, through the bright and dismal circumstances of life, is the essential key in my mission in life for authentic holiness and fruitful perseverance so that God gets the glory. Being happier in God than you are in anything else is the key to holiness and fruitfulness to the glory of God.

The lesson for you: become a Christian Hedonist. Whether you call it that or not doesn't matter. Don't aim at the pleasures of fame. Don't aim at the pleasures of sexual gratification. Don't aim at the pleasures of wealth. Don't aim at the pleasure and contentment and comfort of safety. Aim at all-satisfying joy in God, which will empower you for humility, and chastity, and simplicity, and risk-taking, sacrificial love for other people.

6. I would recognize that I am not my own, that I have been bought with a price, and that I belong, body and soul, to Jesus Christ for his use and his glory.

I would offer myself up to God at age 22 and tell him that he may do with me anything he pleases. He may kill me. He may torture me. He may send me anywhere. He can do me no wrong. He owes me nothing. And I would tell him that any time he pleases, anywhere he pleases, I am his—at his disposal.

And I would memorize Psalm 25, which had a very crucial role for me in seminary. I would memorize Psalm 25 and trust the amazing promises of guidance that are in those precious verses: "Good and upright is the Lord; therefore he instructs sinners in the way. He leads the humble in what is right, and teaches the humble his way"(Psalm 25:8–9).

You don't have to be left to your own wisdom as to what you spend your life doing. If you believe those verses in Psalm 25, he's going to teach you his way for you.

The lesson for you: Memorize Psalm 25. Pray it as your own, and give yourself wholly up to God and his mission. Trust him.

Scripture Index

Genesis

| 1:26–27 | 21 |
| 12:2–3 | 96 |

Exodus

7:3–4	25
14:4	25
20:3–5	26

1 Samuel

| 12:19–20, 20–22 | 28 |

Psalms

1:2	11
16:11	124
19:1	75
22:27	174
23:3	30
25	187
25:8–9	187
25:11	29
42	159
47:1	77
51	159
63:3	50
66:1–2	77
67	94
67:1	95, 104
67:1–2	95, 106
67:2	96, 98
67:3	70, 77, 98, 99
67:3–4	77

67:4	98, 102, 103, 105, 167
67:5	98
67:5–6	109
67:6, 6–7	107
67:7	98
68:32	77
69	159
95:5, 7, 9	161
96	158, 159, 160, 163, 166, 167, 168
96:1	77, 161, 163, 167
96:1–2, 2	166
96:2–3	112, 160
96:3	161, 163, 166, 173
96:4	161, 163
96:10	160, 161
96:13	161
97:1	77
98:4	78
100:1	78
103	159
106:6–8	24

Proverbs

| 21:1 | 103 |

Isaiah

| 12:4 | 173 |

25:1	126, 127, 129
25:1–8	122, 125
25:3	128, 132
25:6, 6–8	127
28:5	20
45:5–6	99
46:9–10	127
48:9–11	75
52:15	11

Ezekiel

20:5–9	23–24
20:8, 9	24
20:13–14	27
36	30, 31
36:22–23	32, 31
36:32	31

Daniel

2:21	103
2:44	75
4:35	104

Habakkuk

2:14	112

Matthew

3:17	22
10:16	153, 178
10:16–18	151
10:16–31	146
10:16–33	150
10:19–20, 20	154
10:21	151
10:22	152, 154

10:23	150, 152, 155
10:25	152, 155, 178
10:26	155
10:28	153, 156
10:29	156
10:31	157
16:18	106, 178
16:24	43
22:43	98
24:9	178
24:14	37, 38, 106, 178
24:35	38
25:23	80
25:35–36	140
28:18	57, 65, 104, 112, 147, 178
28:18–19	57, 178
28:18–20	104, 112, 147
28:19	85, 149, 175
28:19–20	85
28:20	149

Mark

2:17	101
10:45	80

Luke

4:18	140, 142
10:16	101
14:13–14	140
19:9	140
19:10	80
21:16	52, 153
21:16–18	52

John

3:16	112
3:36	149
5:23	100
5:24	156
5:42–43	100
6	60
6:35	79
6:37	59
6:39	44, 59, 65
6:44	59, 60, 65
6:45	101
6:65	59, 60
7:18	31
7:28	100
8:19	100
10	58, 61
10:3–4	58, 59
10:11, 14	58, 60
10:14–15	60
10:16	54, 58, 62, 63, 106
10:26	60
10:27	60, 61
10:27–30	61
10:29	59
11:50	64
11:51–52	39, 64
12:27–28	80
14:7	100
15:11	80
15:16	177
17:3	79
17:4	31
17:6	59, 60
17:9	24, 59
17:13	80
17:24	59
18:9	59
20:21	65, 101

Acts

4:12	174
9	10
14:16	56
16:9	129
16:10–12	130
16:25–34	142
17:26	103
17:30	56
18:9–10	64
19:10	129
20:24	105
20:35	79, 108
22, 26	10
26:18	10

Romans

1:5	74, 119
1:16	14
1:18–21	103
1:18–23	12
1:23	33
2:12	13
2:29	89
3:23	32, 33, 80
3:23–26	33, 80
5:19	102
8:7–8	125
8:28	52
8:30	60
8:35–39	52
9:17	173

10:13	142
10:14–15	143
10:17	174
11:17–27, 33	89
11:36	74
12:20	141
14:4	8
15	6, 7, 10, 11, 15, 32, 39, 76, 111, 148, 175
15:8	32, 39, 76
15:8–9	32, 39, 124, 162
15:9	76, 162, 173
15:9–12	77, 162
15:18–19	15
15:19	14
15:20	7, 12, 15, 111, 148, 175
15:20–21	10, 148
15:21	11
15:22	7
15:23	7, 8, 14
15:24	8, 14
15:28	4

I Corinthians

2:14	17
3:6–8	8
7:7	8
15:58	126

2 Corinthians

1:12	119
1:20	91
2:12–13	114
2:12–17	110, 113
2:14	115, 117
2:15, 15–16	117
2:16	118, 119
2:17	119, 120
3:5	119
7:5–7	115
8:1–2	131
8:2	177
8:9	140
9:7	79
11:4, 5	116
12:11	116

Galatians

1:6	135, 137
1:8	138, 142
1:9, 11–12, 13–14	136
1:15–16	143
1:15–17, 18–22	136
2	137
2:1	137
2:1–10	134
2:2	137
2:3–5	138
2:4	142
2:5	141, 142
2:6, 6–9	138
2:7–9	138–9
2:10	135, 137, 139
3:7, 9, 13–14	97
3:16	96
3:29	97
6:10	141

Ephesians

1:3–6	21
2:3	17
2:7	91
2:12	90
2:12–19	87
2:19	91
3:1–13	84
3:6	189
3:8	85, 90, 92
3:8–9	89, 90
3:8–10	85
3:9	85
3:10	85, 86, 87, 89
5:2	117
6:12	88

Philippians

2:30	44, 45
4:4	79
4:15	131

Colossians

1:16	74
1:24	36, 44, 45, 46
2:15	115

2 Thessalonians

1:9–10	34

2 Timothy

4:5	14, 148

Titus

2:11	105

Hebrews

2:10	74
6	40
6:1, 1–3, 3	40
10:32–33	50
10:34	50, 51
10:35	50
11:38	92
12:2	79
13:5–6	52
13:13	44

1 Peter

1:12	88
3:18	124

1 John

2:23	101
5:12	174

Revelation

2:10	88
5:9	65, 128, 168, 175
5:9–10	38, 168, 175
6:10, 11	41
12:11	178

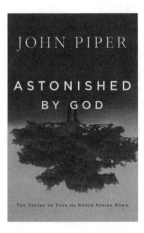

Astonished by God
Ten Truths to Turn the World
Upside Down

John Piper | 192 pages

Turn your world on its head.

bit.ly/AstonishedbyGod

Published for Desiring God by Cruciform Press

An easy read and, according to the author, the closest thing to a systematic theology that he will ever produce.

For more than thirty years, John Piper pastored in the rough and tumble realities of downtown Minneapolis, preaching his people through the ups and down of life one Sunday at a time. When it came to capturing a generation of joy in one final sermon series, he turned to ten trademark truths to leave ringing in his peoples' ears.

These ten are world-shaking truths—each astonishing in its own way. First they turned Piper's own world upside down. Then his church's. And they will continue to turn the whole world upside down as the gospel of Christ advances in distance and depth.

These surprising doctrines, as Piper writes, are "wildly untamable, explosively uncontainable, and electrically future-creating."

Join a veteran author, pastor, and Christian leader as he captures the ten astonishing, compassionate, life-giving, joy-awakening, hope-sustaining truths that have held everything together for him.

(This book is a revised, improved version of Doctrine Matters.*)*

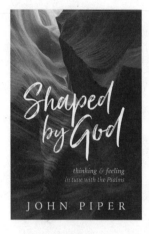

Shaped by God
Thinking and Feeling in Tune with the Psalms

John Piper | 86 pages

**The Psalms are not just commanding...
they are contagious.**

bit.ly/ShapedbyGod

Published for Desiring God by Cruciform Press

God wants your heart.

The whole Bible teaches truth and awakens emotions, but the Psalms are in a category of their own.

They do not just awaken heart; they put it in the foreground. They do not just invite our emotions to respond to God's truth; they put our emotions on display.

The Psalms are not just commanding; they are contagious. We are not just listening to profound ideas and feelings. We are living among them in their overflow.

We touch pillows wet with tears. We hear and feel the unabashed cries of affliction, shame, regret, grief, anger, discouragement, and turmoil. But what makes all this stunningly different from the sorrows of the world is that all of it—absolutely all of it—is experienced in relation to the totally sovereign God.

This book is an invitation. God wants our hearts. He will take them as he finds them.

And then, with the healing contagion of the Psalms, he will shape them. Accept his invitation to come.

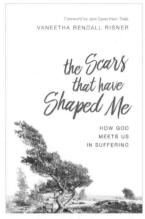

The Scars That Have Shaped Me

How God Meets Us in Suffering

Vaneetha Rendall Risner
Foreword by Joni Eareckson Tada

178 pages

"Raw, transparent, terrifying, and yet amazingly hopeful!"
Brian Fikkert, co-author of *When Helping Hurts*

bit.ly/THESCARS

"Vaneetha writes with creativity, biblical faithfulness, compelling style, and an experiential authenticity that draws other sufferers in. Here you will find both a tested life and a love for the sovereignty of a good and gracious God."
John Piper, author of Desiring God and many other books

"*The Scars That Have Shaped Me* will make you weep and rejoice not just because it brims with authenticity and integrity, but because every page points you to the rest that is found in entrusting your life to one who is in complete control and is righteous, powerful, wise, and good in every way."
Paul Tripp, pastor, author, international conference speaker

"I could not put this book down, except to wipe my tears. Vaneetha's testimony of God's kindness to her in pain was exactly what I needed; no doubt, many others will feel the same. It has helped me process my own grief and loss, and given me renewed hope to care for those in my life who suffer in various ways."
Gloria Furman, author, Missional Motherhood; Alive in Him

"Vaneetha Risner's credibility makes us willing to lean in and listen. Her writing is built on her experience of deep pain, and in the midst of that her rugged determination to hold on to Christ."
Nancy Guthrie, author, Hearing Jesus Speak into Your Sorrow

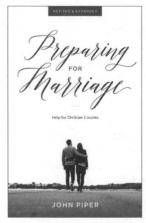

Preparing for Marriage
Help for Christian Couples
(Revised & Expanded Edition)

John Piper | 88 pages

As you prepare for marriage, dare to dream with God.

bit.ly/prep-for-marriage

Published for Desiring God by Cruciform Press

When preparing for marriage, or even in just beginning to consider it, it can be immensely helpful to have the perspective of someone like John Piper, not only a seasoned husband of nearly 50 years, but also a seasoned pastor, careful thinker, and faithful theologian.

Chapter 1 includes John's counsel about engagement, **chapter 2** about wedding planning (and finances).

Chapter 3 provides invaluable instruction about the beautiful, complementary dynamic the Bible teaches between husband and wife.

Sexual relations in marriage is the topic of **chapter 4.**

In **chapter 5,** John helps us ponder how we can guard our marriages in a day in which they are under assault from every side.

Chapter 6 is based on perhaps John Piper's single most important message on marriage. There he goes more macro than many of us have ever dared to go in thinking about what marriage is, and what God designed it for. This is a glorious, true, life-changing vision.

Appendix 1 contains almost 50 questions to ask each other, in 11 categories, and **Appendix 2** addresses hospitality

Happily Ever After
Finding Grace in the Messes of Marriage

John Piper, Francis Chan,
Nancy DeMoss Wolgemuth, and
10 more | 117 pages

**Marriage . . . Harder than you
expected, better than a fairy tale.**

bit.ly/DG-HAPPILY

Published for Desiring God by Cruciform Press

PARTIAL TABLE OF CONTENTS

1. The Goal of Marriage Is Not Marriage – FRANCIS CHAN

2. Seeing Jesus on the Stage of Marriage – P. J. TIBAYAN

3. Serpents, Seeds, and a Savior – NANCY DEMOSS WOLGEMUTH

4. A Special Agent for Change – MARSHALL SEGAL

5. Sex Is for Believers – JOHN PIPER

6. Marital Intimacy Is More Than Sex – JOSH SQUIRES

7. Superior Women—and the Men Who Can't Out-Give Them – DOUGLAS WILSON

8. Good Listening Requires Patience – DAVID MATHIS

9. We Need to Talk about Submission – KIM CASH TATE

10. As Long as Both Shall Live – DAVID MATHIS

11. Unembarrassed by the Bible – JOHN PIPER

12. Do You Expect Your Marriage to Be Easy? – ADRIEN SEGAL

13. The Call to Love and Respect – DOUGLAS WILSON

14. Love Is More Than a Choice – JOHN PIPER

15. Wedded in a Real War – FRANCIS CHAN

16. Five Things Submission Does Not Mean – JOHN PIPER

17. A Possible Marriage-Saver in Nine Steps – JOHN PIPER

The Joy Project
An Introduction to Calvinism

Tony Reinke | 168 pages

**True happiness is not found.
It finds you.**

bit.ly/JOYPROJECT

Published for Desiring God by Cruciform Press

"Biblically, colorfully, and with realistic precision, Tony Reinke presents God's work of saving grace as a jamboree of overwhelming sovereign joy. This is a book of deep truth that does good to the heart as well as the head."
J.I. Packer, Professor, Vancouver, British Columbia

"Our eyes of flesh seek joy in the wrong places, define it with a bankrupt vocabulary, and settle for it using mistaken formulas. All we know to do is try harder and hide our shame, we get stuck and sick, depressed and despondent. This dehumanizes, discourages, and defeats us. But there is hope! *The Joy Project* is applied reformed theology at its best."
Rosaria Champagne Butterfield, Author, The Gospel Comes with a House Key

"A unique and delightful summary of the unfolding drama of God's sovereign grace. Tony, as usual, is biblical, Christ-honoring, gospel-centric, imaginative, and articulate. Who could ask for more? You will enjoy this book!"
Randy Alcorn, Director, Eternal Perspective Ministries

"This is the most beautiful presentation of Calvinism I've ever read."
David Murray, Professor, Puritan Reformed Seminary